STAMPED

RACISM, ANTIRACISM, AND YOU

STAMPED

RACISM, ANTIRACISM, AND YOU

A **REMIX** of the National Book Award-winning
Stamped from the Beginning

Written by
JASON REYNOLDS

Adapted from *Stamped from the Beginning* by and with an introduction from
IBRAM X. KENDI

LITTLE, BROWN AND COMPANY

NEW YORK BOSTON

Little, Brown and Company
Hachette Book Group
1290 Avenue of the Americas, New York, NY 10104
Visit us at LBYR.com

First Edition: March 2020

Little, Brown and Company is a division of Hachette Book Group, Inc. The Little, Brown name and logo are trademarks of Hachette Book Group, Inc.

The publisher is not responsible for websites (or their content) that are not owned by the publisher.

Library of Congress Cataloging-in-Publication Data
Names: Reynolds, Jason, author. | Kendi, Ibram X., author.
Title: Stamped : racism, antiracism, and you / Jason Reynolds and Ibram X. Kendi.
Description: First edition. | New York : Little, Brown and Company, 2020. | "An Adaptation of the National Book Award–winning *Stamped from the Beginning*." | Includes bibliographical references and index. | Audience: Ages 12 and up. | Summary: "A history of racist and antiracist ideas in America, from their roots in Europe until today, adapted from the National Book Award winner *Stamped from the Beginning*." —Provided by publisher.
Identifiers: LCCN 2019033917 | ISBN 9780316453691 (hardcover) | ISBN 9780316453707 (ebook) | ISBN 9780316453677
Subjects: LCSH: Racism—United States—History—Juvenile literature. | United States—Race relations—History—Juvenile literature.
Classification: LCC E184.A1 K346 2020 | DDC 305.800973—dc23
LC record available at https://lccn.loc.gov/2019033917

ISBNs: 978-0-316-45369-1 (hardcover), 978-0-316-45370-7 (ebook)

Printed in Great Britain by Clays Ltd, Elcograf S.p.A.

CLA

To January Hartwell, my great-great-great-grandfather

—JR

To the lives they said don't matter

—IXK

CONTENTS

INTRODUCTION

Dear Reader,

To know the past is to know the present. To know the present is to know yourself.

I write about the history of racism to understand racism today. I want to understand racism today to understand how it is affecting me today. I want you to understand racism today to understand how it is affecting you and America today.

The book you're holding is a remix of my book, *Stamped from the Beginning*, a narrative history of racist and antiracist ideas. A racist idea is any idea that suggests something is wrong or right, superior or inferior, better or worse about a racial group. An antiracist idea is any idea that suggests that racial groups are equals. Racist and antiracist ideas have lived in human minds for nearly six hundred years. Born in western Europe in the mid-1400s, racist ideas traveled to colonial America and have lived in the United States from its beginning. I chronicled their entire life in *Stamped from the Beginning*.

The novelist Jason Reynolds adapted *Stamped from the Beginning* into this book for you. I wish I learned this history at your age. But there were no books telling the complete story of racist ideas. Some books told parts of the story. I hardly wanted to read them, though. Most were so boring, written in ways I could not relate to. But not Jason's books. Not this book. Jason is one of the most gifted writers and thinkers of our time. I don't know of anyone who would have been better at connecting the past to the present for you. Jason is a great writer in the purest sense. A great writer snatches the human eye in the way that a thumping beat snatches the human ear, makes your head bob up and down. It is hard to stop when the beat is on. A great writer makes my head bob from side to side. It is hard to stop when the book is open.

I don't think I'm a great writer like Jason, but I do think I'm a courageous writer. I wrote *Stamped from the Beginning* with my cell phone on, with my television on, with my anger on, with my joy on—always thinking on and on. I watched the televised and untelevised life of the shooting star of #Black Lives Matter during America's stormiest nights. I watched the televised and untelevised killings of unarmed Black human beings at the hands of cops and wannabe cops. I somehow managed to write *Stamped from the Beginning* between the heartbreaking deaths of seventeen-year-old Trayvon Martin and seventeen-year-old Darnesha Harris and twelve-year-old Tamir Rice and sixteen-year-old Kimani Gray and eighteen-year-old Michael Brown, heartbreaks that are a product of America's history of racist ideas as much as a history of racist ideas is a product of these heartbreaks.

Meaning, if not for racist ideas, George Zimmerman would not have thought the hooded Florida teen who liked LeBron James, hip-hop, and *South Park* had to be a robber. Zimmerman's racist ideas in 2012 transformed an easygoing Trayvon Martin walking home from a 7-Eleven holding watermelon juice and Skittles into a menace to society holding danger. Racist ideas cause people to look at an innocent Black face and see a criminal. If not for racist ideas, Trayvon would still be alive. His dreams of becoming a pilot would still be alive.

Young Black males were *twenty-one times* more likely to be killed by police than their White counterparts between 2010 and 2012, according to federal statistics.

The under-recorded, under-analyzed racial disparities between female victims of lethal police force may be even greater. Black people are *five times* more likely to be incarcerated than Whites.

I'm no math whiz, but if Black people make up 13 percent of the US population, then Black people should make up somewhere close to 13 percent of the Americans killed by the police, and somewhere close to 13 percent of the Americans sitting in prisons. But today, the United States remains nowhere close to racial equality. African Americans make up 40 percent of the incarcerated population. These are racial inequities, older than the life of the United States.

Even before Thomas Jefferson and the other founders declared independence in 1776, Americans were arguing over racial inequities, over why they exist and persist, and over why White Americans as a group were prospering more than Black Americans as a group. Historically, there have been three groups involved in this heated argument. Both segregationists and assimilationists, as I call these racist positions in *Stamped from the Beginning*, think Black people are to blame for racial inequity. Both the segregationists and the assimilationists think there is something wrong with Black people and that's why

Black people are on the lower and dying end of racial inequity. The assimilationists believe Black people as a group can be changed for the better, and the segregationists do not. The segregationists and the assimilationists are challenged by *antiracists*. The antiracists say there is nothing wrong or right about Black people and everything wrong with racism. The antiracists say racism is the problem in need of changing, not Black people. The antiracists try to transform racism. The assimilationists try to transform Black people. The segregationists try to get away from Black people. These are the three distinct racial positions you will hear throughout *Stamped: Racism, Antiracism, and You*—the segregationists, the assimilationists, and the antiracists, and how they each have rationalized racial inequity.

In writing *Stamped from the Beginning*, I did not want to just write about racist ideas. I wanted to discover the *source* of racist ideas. When I was in school and first really learning about racism, I was taught the popular origin story. I was taught that ignorant and hateful people had produced racist ideas, and that these racist people had instituted racist policies. But when I learned the motives behind the production of racist ideas, it became obvious that this folktale, though sensible, was not true. I found that the need of powerful people to defend racist policies that benefited them led them to produce racist ideas, and when unsuspecting people consumed these racist ideas, they became ignorant and hateful.

Think of it this way. There are only two potential explanations for racial inequity, for why White people were free and Black people were enslaved in the United States. Either racist policies forced Black people into enslavement, or animalistic Black people were fit for slavery. Now, if you make a lot of money enslaving people, then to defend your business you want people to believe that Black people are fit for slavery. You will produce and circulate this racist idea to stop abolitionists from challenging slavery, from abolishing what is making you rich. You see the racist policies of slavery arrive first and then racist ideas follow to justify slavery. And these racist ideas make people ignorant about racism and hateful of racial groups.

When I began writing *Stamped from the Beginning*, I must confess that I held quite a few racist ideas. Yes, me. I'm an African American. I'm a historian of African Americans. But it's important to remember that racist ideas are ideas. Anyone can produce them or consume them, as this book shows. I thought there were certain things wrong with Black people (and other racial groups). Fooled by racist ideas, I did not fully realize that the only thing wrong with Black people is that we think something is wrong with Black people. I did not fully realize that the only thing extraordinary about White people is that they think something is extraordinary about White people. There are lazy, hardworking, wise, unwise, harmless, and harmful *individuals* of every race, but no racial *group* is better or worse than another racial group in any way.

Committed to this antiracist idea of group equality, I was able to discover, self-critique, and shed the racist ideas I had consumed over my lifetime while I uncovered and exposed the racist ideas that others have produced over the lifetime of America. The first step to building an antiracist America is acknowledging America's racist past. By acknowledging America's racist past, we can acknowledge America's racist present. In acknowledging America's racist present, we can work toward building an antiracist America. An antiracist America where no racial group has more or less, or is thought of as more or less. An antiracist America where the people no longer hate on racial groups or try to change racial groups. An antiracist America where our skin color is as irrelevant as the colors of the clothes over our skin.

And an antiracist America is sure to come. No power lasts forever. There will come a time when Americans will *realize* that the only thing wrong with Black people is that they think something is wrong with Black people. There will come a time when racist ideas will no longer obstruct us from seeing the complete and utter abnormality of racial disparities. There will come a time when we will love humanity, when we will gain the courage to fight for an equitable society for our beloved humanity, knowing, intelligently, that when we fight for humanity, we are fighting for ourselves. There will come a time. Maybe, just maybe, that time is now.

In solidarity,

Ibram X. Kendi

SECTION

1

1415–1728

CHAPTER 1

The Story of the World's First Racist

BEFORE WE BEGIN, LET'S GET SOMETHING STRAIGHT. This is not a history book. I repeat, this is *not* a history book. At least not like the ones you're used to reading in school. The ones that feel more like a list of dates (there will be some), with an occasional war here and there, a declaration (*definitely* gotta mention that), a constitution (that too), a court case or two, and, of course, the paragraph that's read during Black History Month (Harriet! Rosa! Martin!). This isn't that. This isn't a history book. Or, at least, it's not that kind of history book. Instead, what this is, is a book that contains history. A history directly connected to our lives as we live them right this minute. This is a present book. A book about the here and now. A book that hopefully will help us better understand why we are where we are as Americans, specifically as our identity pertains to race.

Uh-oh. The R-word. Which for many of us still feels rated R. Or can be matched only with another R word—*run*. But don't. Let's all just take a deep breath. Inhale. Hold it. Exhale and breathe out:

R A C E.

See? Not so bad. Except for the fact that race has been a strange and persistent poison in American history, which I'm sure you already know. I'm also sure that, depending on where you are and where you've grown up, your experiences with it—or at least the moment in which you recognize it—may vary. Some may believe race isn't an issue anymore, that it's a thing of the past, old tales of bad times. Others may be certain that race is like an alligator, a dinosaur that never went extinct but instead evolved. And though hiding in murky swamp waters, that leftover monster is still deadly. And then there are those of you who know that race and, more critical, racism are *everywhere*. Those of you who see racism regularly robbing people of liberty, whether as a violent stickup or as a sly pickpocket. The thief known as racism is all around. This book, this *not history* history book, this present book, is meant to take you on a race journey from then to now, to show why we feel how we feel, why we live how we live, and why this poison, whether recognizable or unrecognizable, whether it's a scream or a whisper, just won't go away.

This isn't the be-all end-all. This isn't the whole meal. It's more like an appetizer. Something in preparation for the feast to come. Something to get you excited about choosing your seat—the right seat—at the table.

Oh! And there are three words I want you to keep in mind. Three words to describe the people we'll be exploring:

Segregationists. Assimilationists. Antiracists.

There are serious definitions to these things, but... I'm going to give you mine.

Segregationists are haters. Like, *real* haters. People who hate you for not being like them. Assimilationists are people who like you, but only with quotation marks. Like..."like" you. Meaning, they "like" you because you're like them. And then there are antiracists. They *love* you because you're like you. But it's important to note, life can rarely be wrapped into single-word descriptions. It isn't neat and perfectly shaped. So sometimes, over the course of a lifetime (and even over the course of a day), people can take on and act out ideas represented by more than one of these three identities. Can be *both, and.* Just keep that in mind as we explore these folks.

And, actually, these aren't just the words we'll be using to describe the people in this book. They're also the words we'll be using to describe you. And me. All of us.

So where do we start? We might as well just jump in and begin with the world's first racist. I know what you're thinking. You're thinking, *How could anyone know who the world's first racist was?* Or you're thinking, *Yeah, tell us, so we can find out where he lives.* Well, he's dead. Been dead for six hundred years. Thankfully. And before I tell you about him, I have to give you a little context.

Europe. That's where we are. Where he was. As I'm sure you've learned by now, the Europeans (Italians, Portuguese, Spanish, Dutch, French, British) were conquering everyone, because if there's one thing all history books *do* say, it's that Europeans conquered the majority of the world. The year is 1415, and Prince Henry (there's always a Prince Henry) convinced his father, King John of Portugal, to basically pull a caper and capture the main Muslim trading depot on the northeastern tip of Morocco. Why? Simple. Prince Henry was jealous. The Muslims had riches, and if Prince Henry could get the Muslims out of the way, then those riches and resources could be easily accessed. Stolen. A jack move. A robbery. Plain and simple. The take, a bountiful supply of gold. And Africans. That's right, the Portuguese were capturing Moorish people, who would become prisoners of war in a war the Moors hadn't planned on fighting but had to, to survive. And by prisoners, I mean property. Human property.

But neither Prince Henry nor King John of Portugal was given the title *World's First Racist*, because the truth is, capturing people wasn't an unusual thing back then. Just a fact of life. That illustrious moniker would go to a man named neither Henry nor John but something way more awesome, who did something *not* awesome at all—Gomes Eanes de Zurara. Zurara, which sounds like a cheerleader chant, did just that. Cheerleaded? Cheerled? Whatever. He was a cheerleader. Kind of. Not the kind who roots for a team and pumps up a crowd, but he *was* a man who made sure the team he played for was represented and heralded as great. He made sure Prince Henry was looked at as a brilliant quarterback making ingenious plays, and that every touchdown was the mark of a superior player. How did Zurara do this? Through literature. Storytelling.

He wrote the story, a biography of the life and slave trading of Prince Henry. Zurara was an obedient commander in Prince Henry's Military Order of Christ and would eventually complete his book, which would become the first defense of African slave trading. It was called *The Chronicle of the Discovery and Conquest of Guinea*. In it, Zurara bragged about the Portuguese being early in bringing enslaved Africans from the Western Sahara Cape, and spoke about owning humans as if they were exclusive pairs of sneakers. Again, this was common. But he *upped* the brag by also explaining what made Portugal different from their European neighbors in terms of slave trading. The Portuguese now saw enslaving people as missionary work. A mission from God to help civilize and Christianize the African "savages." At least, that's what Zurara claimed. And the reason this was a one-up on his competitors, the Spanish and Italians, was because they were still enslaving eastern Europeans, as in White people (not called White people back then). Zurara's ace, his trick shot, was that the Portuguese had enslaved Africans (of all shades, by the way) supposedly for the purpose of saving their wretched souls.

Zurara made Prince Henry out to be some kind of youth minister canvassing the street, doing community work, when what Prince Henry really was, was more of a gangster. More of a shakedown man, a kidnapper getting a commission for bringing the king captives. Prince Henry's cut, like a finder's fee: 185 slaves, equaling money, money, money, though it was always framed as a noble cause, thanks to Zurara, who was also paid for his pen. Seems like Zurara was just a liar, right? A fiction writer? So, what makes him the world's first racist? Well, Zurara was the first person to *write* about and *defend* Black human ownership, and this single document began the recorded history of anti-Black racist ideas. You know how the kings are always attached to where they rule? Like, King John of Portugal? Well, if Gomes Eanes de Zurara was the king of anything (which he wasn't), he would've been King Gomes of Racism.

Zurara's book, *The Chronicle of the Discovery and Conquest of Guinea*, was a hit. And you know what hits do—they spread. Like a pop song that everyone claims to hate, but everyone knows the words to, and then suddenly no one hates the song anymore, and instead it becomes an anthem. Zurara's book became an anthem. A song sung all across Europe as the primary source of knowledge on unknown Africa and African peoples for the original slave traders and enslavers in Spain, Holland, France, and England.

Zurara depicted Africans as savage animals that needed taming. This depiction over time would even begin to convince some African people that they were inferior, like al-Hasan Ibn Muhammad al-Wazzan al-Fasi, a well-educated Moroccan who was on a diplomatic journey along the Mediterranean Sea when he was captured and enslaved. He was eventually freed by Pope Leo X, who converted him to Christianity, renamed him Johannes Leo (he later become known as Leo Africanus, or Leo the African), and possibly commissioned him to write a survey of Africa. And in that survey, Africanus echoed Zurara's sentiments of Africans, his own people. He said they were hypersexual savages, making him the first known African racist. When I was growing up, we called this "drinking the Kool-Aid" or "selling out." Either way, Zurara's documentation of the racist idea that Africans needed slavery in order to be fed and taught Jesus, and that it was all ordained by God, began to seep in and stick to the European cultural psyche. And a few hundred years later, this idea would eventually reach America.

CHAPTER 2

Puritan Power

OKAY, SO BY NOW HOPEFULLY YOU'RE SAYING, *WOW, THIS really isn't like the history books I'm used to.* And if you aren't saying that, well...you're a liar. And, guess what, you wouldn't be the first.

After Gomes Eanes de Zurara's ridiculous, money-grabbing lie, there were other European "race theorists" who followed suit, using his text as a jumping-off point for their own concepts and racist ideas to justify the enslavement of Africans. Because if there's one thing we all know about humans, it's that most of us are followers, looking for something to be part of to make us feel better about our own selfishness. Or is that just me? Just me? Got it. Anyway, the followers came sniffing around, drumming up their own cockamamie (best word ever, even better than Zurara, though possibly a synonym) theories, two of which would set the table for the conversation around racism for centuries to come.

Those theories were:

1. **C L I M A T E   T H E O R Y :**
   This actually came from Aristotle (we'll get back to him later), who questioned whether Africans were born "this way" or if the heat of the continent made them inferior. Many agreed it was climate, and that if African people lived in cooler temperatures, they could, in fact, become White. And,

2. **C U R S E   T H E O R Y :**
   In 1577, after noticing that Inuit people in northeastern (freezing-cold) Canada were darker than the people living in the hotter south, English travel writer George Best determined—conveniently for all parties interested in owning slaves—that it couldn't have been climate that made darker people inferior, and instead determined that Africans were, in fact, cursed. (First of all, could you imagine someone on the Travel Channel tell-

ing you that you're cursed? Like...really?) And what did Best use to prove this theory? Only one of the most irrefutable books of the time: the Bible. In Best's whimsical interpretation of the book of Genesis, Noah orders his White sons not to have sex with their wives on the ark, and then tells them that the first child born after the flood would inherit the earth. When the evil, tyrannical, and hypersexual Ham (goes HAM and) has sex on the ark, God wills that Ham's descendants will be dark and disgusting, and the whole world will look at them as symbols of trouble. Simply put, Ham's kids would be Black and bad, ultimately making Black... bad. Curse theory would become the anchor of what would justify American slavery.

It would branch off into another ridiculous idea, the strange concept that because Africans were cursed and because, according to these Europeans, they needed enslavement in order to be saved and civilized, the relationship between slave and master was loving. That it was more like parent and child. Or minister and member. Mentor, mentee. They were painting a compassionate picture about what was certainly a terrible experience, because, well, human beings were being forced into servitude, and there's no way to spin that into one big happy family.

But the literature said otherwise. That's right, there was another piece of literature, this one written by a man named William Perkins, called *Ordering a Familie*, published in 1590, in which he argued that the slave was just part of a loving family unit that was ordered a particular way. And that the souls and the potential of the souls were equal, but not the skin. It's like saying, "I look at my dog like I look at my children, even though I've trained my dog to fetch my paper by beating it and yanking its leash." But the idea of it all let the new enslavers off the emotional hook and portrayed them as benevolent do-gooders "cleaning up" the Africans.

A generation later, slavery touched down in the newly colonized America. And the people there to usher it in and, more important, to use it to build this new country were two men, each of whom saw himself as a similar kind of do-gooder. Their names, John Cotton and Richard Mather.

About Cotton and Mather. They were Puritans.

About Puritans. They were English Protestants who believed the reformation of the Church of England was basically watering down Christianity, and they sought to regulate it to keep it more disciplined and rigid. So, these two men, at different times, traveled across the Atlantic in search of a new land (which would be Boston) where they could escape English persecution and preach their version—a "purer" version—of Christianity. They landed in America after treacherous trips, especially Richard Mather, whose ship sailed into a storm in 1635 and almost collided with a massive rock in the ocean. Mather, of course, saw his survival of this journey to America as a miracle, and became even more devoted to God.

Both men were ministers. They built churches in Massachusetts but, more important, they built systems. The church wasn't just a place of worship. The church was a place of power and influence, and in this new land, John Cotton and Richard Mather had a whole lot of power and influence. And the first thing they did to spread the Puritan way was find other people who were like-minded. And with those like-minded folks, they created schools to enforce higher education skewed toward their way of thinking.

What school, do you think, was the first to get the Puritan touch? This is a trick question. Because the answer is the very first university in America, *ever* (remember, this society is all brand-new!). And the very first university in America *ever* was Harvard University. But a tricky thing happens with the opening of Harvard. A thing that directly connects to Zurara, and the curse and climate theories and everything we've talked about thus far. See, Cotton and Mather were students of Aristotle. And Aristotle, though held up as one of the greatest Greek philosophers of all time, famous for things we will not be discussing here because this is not a history book, believed something else he's not nearly as famous for. And that's his belief in human hierarchy.

Aristotle believed that Greeks were superior to non-Greeks. John Cotton and Richard Mather took Aristotle's idea (because they, too, were followers) and flipped it into a new equation, substituting "Puritan" for "Greek." And because of their miraculous journeys across the raging ocean, especially Richard Mather's, they believed they were a chosen people. Special in the eyes of God. Puritan superiority.

According to the Puritans, they were better than:

1. Native Americans.

2. Anglican (English) people who weren't Puritans.

3. Everyone else who wasn't a Puritan.

4. Especially African people.

And guess what they did during the development of Harvard? They made it so that Greek and Latin texts could not be disputed. Which meant Aristotle, a man who believed in human hierarchy and used climate to justify *which* humans were better, could not be disputed, and instead had to be taken as truth.

And just like that, the groundwork was laid not only for slavery to be justified but for it to be justified for a long, long time, simply because it was woven into the religious *and* educational systems of America. All that was needed to complete this oppressive puzzle was slaves.

America at this time was like one of those games where you have to build a world. A social network of farmers and planters. And if you weren't a farmer-planter, then you were a missionary. So, you were either dirt folk or church folk, everyone working to grow on stolen land— obviously their native neighbors weren't happy about any of this, because their world was being broken, while a new world was being built, planted one seed at a time.

That seed? Tobacco. A man named John Pory (a defender of curse theory), the cousin of one of the early major landowners, was named America's first legislative leader. First thing he did was set the price of tobacco, seeing as it would be the country's cash crop. But if tobacco was really going to bring in some money, if it was really going to be the natural resource used to power the country, then they would need more *human* resource to grow it.

See where this is going?

In August 1619, a Spanish ship called the *San Juan Bautista* was hijacked by two pirate ships. The *Bautista* was carrying 350 Angolans, because Latin American slaveholders had already figured out their own slave-trading system and had enslaved 250,000 people. The pirates robbed the *Bautista*, taking sixty of the Angolans. They headed east, eventually coming upon the shores of Jamestown, Virginia. They sold twenty Angolans to that cousin of John Pory. The one with all the land, who happened also to be the governor of Virginia. His name was George Yeardley, and those first twenty slaves, for Yeardley and Pory, were right on time... to work.

But remember, America was full of planters and missionaries. And the new slaves would cause a bit of conflict between the two. For the planter, the slave was a big help and could be the four-digit code to the American ATM. Here comes the cash. On the flip side, missionaries—coming down the line of Puritanism and Zurara's propaganda—felt slavery was a means to salvation. Planters wanted to grow profits, while missionaries wanted to grow God's kingdom.

No one cared what the enslaved African wanted (which, to start, would've been not to be enslaved). They definitely didn't want the religion of their masters. And their masters resisted, too. Enslavers weren't interested in hearing anything about converting their slaves. Saving their crops each year was more important to them than saving souls. It was harvest over humanity. And the excuses they gave to avoid baptizing slaves were:

Africans were too barbaric to be converted.

Africans were savage at the soul.

Africans couldn't be loved

EVEN BY GOD.

CHAPTER 3

A Different Adam

As I mentioned before, after Zurara's nonsense documentation about slave trading and the savage nature of Africans, many other Europeans started to write their *own* testimonies and theories. But it didn't stop with just Aristotle or George Best (the travel writer). A century later, the tradition—one that would go on indefinitely—of writing about the African was alive and well and more creative than ever. And when I say creative, I mean trash.

There was a piece in 1664 by the British minister Richard Baxter called *A Christian Directory*.

NOTES ON BAXTER:
He believed slavery was helpful for African people. He even said there were "voluntary slaves," as in Africans who *wanted* to be slaves so that they could be baptized. (Voluntary slaves? Richard Baxter was clearly out of his mind.)

There was also work by the great English philosopher John Locke.

NOTES ON LOCKE (in regard to African people):
He believed that the most unblemished, purest, perfect minds belonged to Whites, which basically meant Africans had dirty brains.

And by the Italian philosopher Lucilio Vanini.

NOTES ON VANINI:
He believed Africans were born of a "different Adam," and had a different creation story. Of course, this would mean they were a different species. It was kind of like saying (or

to him, *proving*) that Africans weren't actually human. Like they were maybe animals, or monsters, or aliens, but not human—at least not like Whites—and therefore didn't have to be treated as such. This theory, which is called polygenesis, broke the race conversation wide open. It took Zurara's initial benevolent-master mess and put it in bold. Like, Africans went from savages to **SAVAGES**, which revved up the necessity for Christian conversion and civilizing.

P A U S E.

I know we've been going on and on about the people working to justify slavery, but it's important (very important) to note that there were also people all along the way who stood up and fought against these ridiculously racist ideas with abolitionist ideas. In this particular case, the case of Vanini's theory of polygenesis, a group of Mennonites in Germantown, Pennsylvania, rose up. The Mennonites were a Christian denomination from the German- and Dutch-speaking areas of central Europe. During the sixteenth and early seventeenth centuries, orthodox authorities were killing them for their religious beliefs. Mennonites didn't want to leave behind one place of oppression to build another in America, so they circulated an antislavery petition on April 18, 1688, denouncing oppression due to skin color by equating it with oppression due to religion. Both oppressions were wrong. This petition—the 1688 Germantown Petition Against Slavery—was the first piece of writing that was **antiracist** (word check!) among European settlers in colonial America.

But whenever people rise up against bad things, bad things tend to get worse. You know the old saying, *When the going gets tough, the tough get...racist.* Or something like that. So, all that antiracist talk coming from the Mennonites was shut down because slaveholders didn't like their business talked about like it was wrong.

Because they needed their slaves.

Because their slaves made them money.

It's really all quite simple.

Now there's an obvious backdrop we need to discuss—the subject of our first-grade, color-in-the-lines cornucopia worksheets. The misinterpreted, misrepresented owners of this terrain—the Native Americans. All this is happening on their land. A land that was taken from them forcefully, claimed and owned by Europeans running from their homelands, afraid for their lives. It's kind of like the kid who gets beat up every day at school, comes home crying to his mother, and she decides to take him to a new school. And guess what he does when he gets to the new school? He pretends like he wasn't just on the receiving end of a boot sole and instead becomes the most annoying tough guy in the world. And the Native Americans were sick of the tough-acting, arrogant new kid.

So...*FIGHT!*

The Native American and new (White) American beef had been brewing for over a year (but let's be honest, it had to have been brewing *much* longer than that). And when I say brewing, I mean...people were dying. Bloodshed in the soil. The Puritans in New England had already lost homes and dozens of soldiers. But eventually a man named Metacomet, a Native American war leader, was killed, which basically ended the battle in 1676. Puritans cut up his body (like...savages?) as if it were a hog's, and paraded his remains around Plymouth.

But Metacomet's tribe weren't the only indigenous people, obviously. Or the only ones being attacked. Down in Virginia, a twenty-nine-year-old frontier planter, Nathaniel Bacon...Wait. Let's take a time-out and acknowledge the irony in the fact that there was a *planter* whose last name was *bacon*. Bacon! Maybe he should've been a butcher! Anyway, Bacon was upset not about the race issue but instead about the class issue. Here he was, a White laborer who was also being taken advantage of by the White elite. So, what he did to disrupt the powers that be was shift his anger from the rich Whites to the Susquehannocks, a tribe of Natives. This may seem like a strange move, but it was a smart play because the governor at the time, William Berkeley, was doing anything he could *not* to fight with the Natives, because it would mess up his fur trade, and thus mess up his money. So, attacking the Natives was a way of attacking the power structure, but through the back door. As we say now, "Hit 'em in their pockets, where it *really* hurts." And to make matters worse, Bacon declared liberty for all servants and Blacks, because, as far as he was concerned, though they were different races, they were the same class and should be united against the true enemy—rich Whites. But the governor knew if Blacks and Whites joined forces, he'd be done. Everything would be done. It would've been an apocalypse. So, he had to devise a way to turn poor Whites and poor Blacks against each other, so that they'd be forever separated and unwilling to join hands and raise fists against the elite. And the way he did this was by creating (wait for it...) White privileges.

Time for a breath break. Everyone inhale. Hold it. Exhale and breathe it out:

PRIVILEGE.

Still here? Good. Let's move on.

So, White privileges were created, and, at this time, they included:

1. Only the White rebels were pardoned; legislators prescribed thirty lashes for any slave who lifted a hand "against any Christian" (Christian now meant White).

2. All Whites now wielded absolute power to abuse any African person.

Those are the two most important ones—poor Whites wouldn't be punished, but they could surely do the punishing.

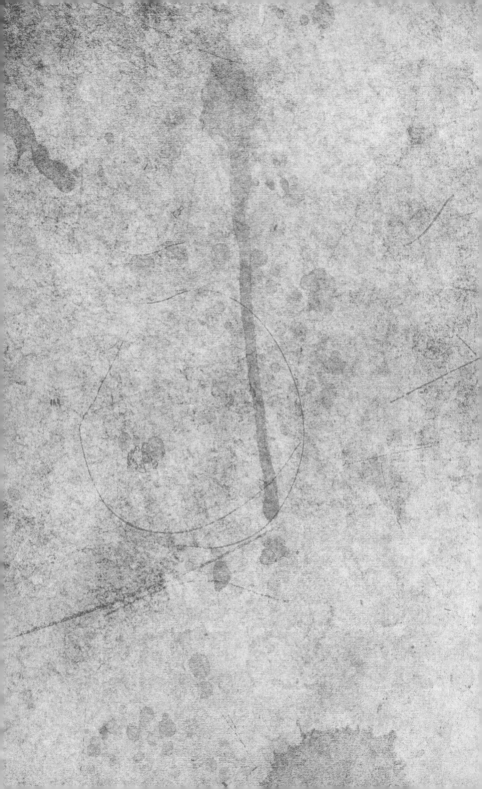

CHAPTER 4

A Racist Wunderkind

REMEMBER JOHN COTTON AND RICHARD MATHER, the Puritans who got the American race ball rolling? Well, turns out they had a grandson. Well, not the two of them together, obviously, but:

Richard Mather's wife dies.

John Cotton dies.

Richard Mather marries John Cotton's widow, Sarah.

Richard Mather's youngest son, Increase, marries Sarah's daughter, Maria, making her his wife and stepsister. (Umm...)

Increase and Maria have a son. February 12, 1663. They name him after both families.

Cotton and Mather becomes...Cotton Mather.

By the time Cotton Mather heard about Bacon's Rebellion, he was already in college. An eleven-year-old Harvard student (the youngest of all time), he was obviously a nerd, and on top of all that, he was extremely religious. He knew he was special, or at least meant to be, which of course did nothing but fill his fellow classmates with spite. They wanted desperately to break him down, make him sin. Because no one likes a show-off. Basically, Cotton Mather was obsessed with being perfect and blamed himself for everything wrong or different with him, believing even his stutter, with which he struggled, was due to something sinful he'd done.

Because he was so insecure about his speech impediment, Cotton Mather took to writing, and eventually he would write more sermons than any other Puritan in history. By the time he graduated from Harvard, he'd overcome his stutter, which to him was, of course, a deliverance from God.

Being delivered from his stutter was a good thing, because he was destined for the pulpit. The grandson of two Puritan preachers *had* to grow up to be one. No other choice. And there was no better way to begin his career as a clergyman than for him to co-pastor his father's (also a preacher) church. But while he was avoiding his bullies at

Harvard, trying to use his words and doing anything he could to walk a righteous path in the eyes of God, there was a tension brewing between New England and "Old" England. In 1676, an English colonial administrator, Edward Randolph, had journeyed to New England to see the damage done by Metacomet, the indigenous war hero, and his warriors. Randolph reported this back to King Charles II and suggested they tighten the grip around New England because, clearly, the New World experiment wasn't going so well. So now big brother was threatening to step in and clean up little brother's mess, which meant Massachusetts would lose local rule if it didn't defy the king. Of course, the other option was for the colonists to just fall in line. But that would mean giving up everything they'd worked to build. Defiance seemed like a stronger play. And in 1689, New Englanders did just that.

The thing about revolution is that it almost always has to do with poor people angry about being manipulated by the rich. So, Cotton Mather, though a recent graduate of Harvard and a God-fearing, sermonizing, well-read man, had a problem on his hands because...he was rich. He'd come from an elite family, gotten an elite education, and lived an elite, though pious, life, far from the planters and even farther from the slaves. So, the Revolution of 1688, which was called the Glorious Revolution, was not so glorious for him. And, fearing that the anger that caused the uprising would go from the British elites to the elites right at home—meaning him—he created a new villain as a distraction. An invisible demon (cue the scary music).

Mather wrote a book called *Memorable Providences, Relating to Witchcrafts and Possessions*. That's right, Cotton Mather, the genius boy, destined for intellectual and spiritual greatness, was obsessed with witches. And this obsession would set a fire he couldn't have seen coming, but welcomed as the will of God.

Mather's book, outlining the symptoms of witchcraft, reflected his crusade against the enemies of White souls. His father was just as obsessed, but no one poured gasoline on the witchy fire like a minister in Salem, Massachusetts, named Samuel Parris. In 1692, when Parris's nine-year-old daughter suffered convulsions and chokes, he believed she'd been possessed or cursed by a witch.

That was all it took. The witch hunt began.

Over the next few months, as bewitching instances continued to happen, people continued to be accused of witchcraft, which, luckily for folks like Cotton Mather, turned attention away from the political and onto the religious. And in nearly every instance, "the devil" who was preying upon innocent White Puritans was described as Black. Of course. One Puritan accuser described the devil as "a little black bearded man"; another saw "a black thing of a considerable bigness." A Black thing jumped in one man's window. "The body was like that of a Monkey," the observer added. "The Feet like a Cocks, but the Face much like a man's." Since the devil represented criminality, and since criminals in New England were said to be the devil's minions, the Salem witch hunt made the Black face the face of criminality. It was like racist algebra. Solve for x. Solve for White. Solve for anything other than truth.

Once the witch hunt eventually died down, the Massachusetts authorities apologized to the accused, reversed the convictions of the trials, and provided reparations in the early 1700s. But Cotton Mather never stopped defending the Salem witch trials, because he never stopped defending the religious, slaveholding, gender, class, and racial hierarchies reinforced by the trials. He saw himself as the defender of God's law and the crucifier of any non-Puritan, African, Native American, poor person, or woman who defied God's law by not submitting to it.

And just as it went with the theorists who came before him—the racist children of Zurara—Cotton Mather's ideas and writings spread from Massachusetts throughout the land. This was just as two other things were happening: Boston was becoming the intellectual capital of the new America, and tobacco was taking off. Booming. Which meant *more* slaves were needed in order to manage it.

As the population of enslaved people grew, which is what slaveholders needed in order to till the land and grow the tobacco for free, the fear of more revolt grew with it. Seems like a natural fear in response to such an unnatural system. So, in order to keep their human property from rising up, slaveholders and politicians created a *new* unnatural system. A new set of racist codes.

1. No interracial relationships.

2. Tax imported captives.

3. Classify Natives and Blacks the same way you would horses and hogs in the tax code. Meaning, they were literally classified as livestock, and not as human.

4. Blacks can't hold office.

5. All property owned by a slave is sold, which of course contributes to Black poverty.

6. Oh, and White indentured servants who were freed are awarded fifty acres of property, of course contributing to White prosperity.

And while all this was going on—all this systemic knife turning, all this racist political play, all the violence and discrimination—Cotton Mather, all high and mighty, was still trying to convince people that the only thing necessary, the only mission of slavery, had to be to save the souls of the slaves, because through that salvation the enslaved would in turn be whitened. *Purified.*

Enslavers became more open to these ideas over time, right up until the First Great Awakening, which swept through the colonies in the 1730s, spearheaded by a Connecticut man named Jonathan Edwards. Edwards, whose father had studied under Increase Mather, was a direct descendant of the Mathers' Puritan thought. He spoke about human equality (in soul) and the capability of everyone for conversion. And as this racist Christian awakening continued to evolve, as people like Edwards carried on the torch of torture, Cotton Mather continued to age. In 1728, on his sixty-fifth birthday, he called his church's pastor into the room for prayer. The next day, Cotton Mather, one of New England's greatest God-fearing scholars, was dead. But you know how death is. Your body goes, but your ideas don't. Your impact lingers on, even when it's poisonous. Some bodies get put into the ground and daisies bloom. Others encourage the sprouting of weeds, weeds that work to strangle whatever's living and growing around them.

SECTION

2

1743–1826

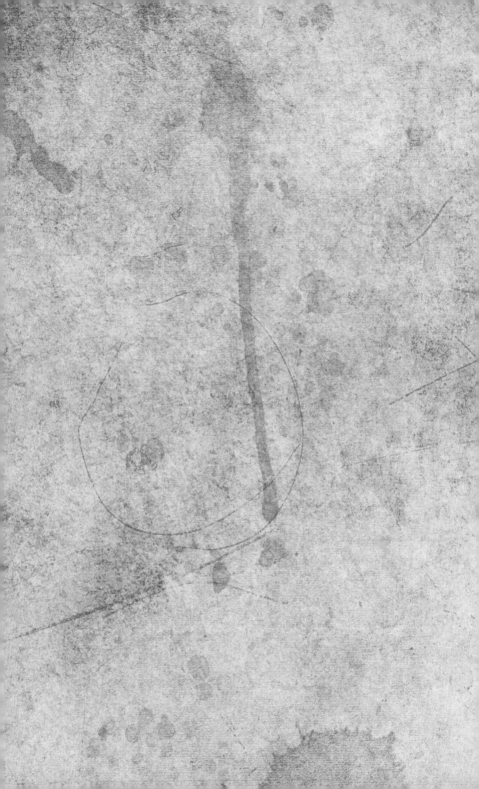

CHAPTER 5

Proof in the Poetry

THIS IS THE WAY LIFE WORKS. THINGS GROW AND change, or at least things *seem* to change. Sometimes the change is in name only; sometimes there's a fundamental shift. Most times it's a bit of both. In the mid-1700s, after Cotton Mather's death and in the midst of his followers' continuing his legacy, the new America entered what we now call the Enlightenment era.

Enlightenment. What does it mean? Well, according to our old pals Merriam and Webster, *enlightenment* is defined as "the act or means of enlightening: the state of being enlightened." (Isn't it funny how every teacher has always told you not to define a word by using the word in the definition? Hey, next time, just say, "If the folks who wrote the dictionary can do it, so can I!") But to be enlightened just means to be informed. To be free from ignorance. So, this new movement, the Enlightenment, was megaphoning the fact that there was a new generation, a new era that knew more. Better thinkers. And in America the leader of this "better thinkers" movement was Mr. One-Hundred-Dollar Bill himself—Benjamin Franklin.

Franklin started a club called the American Philosophical Society in 1743 in Philadelphia. It was modeled after the Royal Society in England, and served as, basically, a club for smart (White) people. Thinkers. Philosophers. And...racists. See, in the Enlightenment era, light was seen as a metaphor for intelligence (think, *I see the light*) and also whiteness (think, opposite of dark). And this is what Franklin was bringing to America through his club of ingenious fools. And one of those walking contradictions was Thomas Jefferson.

About Jefferson. You know how I said Gomes Eanes de Zurara was the world's first racist? Well, Thomas Jefferson might've been the world's first White person to say, "I have Black friends." I don't know if that's true, but I'm willing to make the bet. He was raised nonreligious, in a house where Native Americans were houseguests, and Black people, though slaves, were his friends, as far as he could tell. As a young man, he didn't think of them as less or consider slavery much at all. As a matter of fact, Jefferson didn't even really see them as slaves. It wasn't until he was older, when his African "friends" started telling him about the horrors of slavery—including the terror in his own home—that he realized their lives were more different than he'd ever known. And how could they not be? His father owned the second-largest number of enslaved people in Albemarle County, Virginia, and I don't know about you all, but I don't *own* my friends.

As Thomas Jefferson grew up, he studied law to grapple with antiracist thought (yes, the slave owner was studying *anti*racism). He eventually went on to build his own plantation, in Charlottesville, Virginia, putting money over morals, a lesson learned from his father. Slavery wasn't about people, it was about profit. Business.

I often wonder if there were times on Jefferson's plantation when one of his slaves—one of his *friends*— taught him things he couldn't learn from the American Philosophical Society. And, if so, if that particular slave was seen as someone, something, different. Like a "Super Black." And if his "I have Black friends" was ever followed up with, "You're not like the rest of them."

And if when Jefferson's friends came over, he had that slave showcase his intelligence or his talent or whatever "special" thing he thought only White people could do. Because up the coast, in Boston, during the time that Jefferson was building his plantation, a young woman named Phillis Wheatley was under a microscope, for being "special."

Not, like, literally under a microscope. She was too big for that. Not microscopic at all. As a matter of fact, she was being studied not because she was small but rather because she had an intellectual and creative bigness that White people couldn't believe.

She was a poet. But before she was a poet, she was a young girl, a captive brought over on a ship from Senegambia. She was purchased by the Wheatley family, who wanted a daughter to replace the one they'd lost. Phillis would be that stand-in. And because she was a "daughter," she was actually never a working slave and was even homeschooled.

By eleven, she'd written her first poem.

By twelve, she could read Greek and Latin classics, English literature, and the Bible.

That same year she also published her first poem.

By fifteen, she'd written a poem about wanting to go to Harvard, which was all male and all White.

By nineteen, she began gathering her poems into a collection. A book.

By now, you know there was no way she was going to get published. At least not without jumping through some serious hoops. So, in 1772, John Wheatley, Phillis's adoptive father, got eighteen of the smartest men in America together in Boston so that they could test her. See if a Black person could really be as intelligent and literate as Phillis. As they were. And, of course, she answered every question correctly and proved herself... human.

Still, no one would publish her. I mean, those eighteen men knew she was brilliant, but none of them were publishers, and even if they were, why would they risk their businesses by publishing a Black girl in the midst of a racist world where poetry was for and by rich White people?

But Wheatley's achievements still proved a point, that Black people weren't dumb, and this information became ammo for people who were antislavery. People like Benjamin Rush, a physician from Philadelphia who wrote a pamphlet saying that Black people weren't born savages but instead were made savages *by* slavery.

Record scratch.

P A U S E.

Okay, let's just get something straight, because this is an argument you will hear over and over again through life (I hope not, but probably). To say that slavery—or, in today's time, poverty—*makes* Black people animals or subhuman is racist. I know, I know. It seems to be coming from a "good" place. Like, when people say, "You're cute...for a (insert physical attribute that shouldn't be used as an insult but is definitely used as an insult because it doesn't fit with the strange and narrow European standard of beauty)." It's underhanded and still doesn't recognize you for you. It's the difference between an **assimilationist** and an **antiracist** (word check!).

So, when it came to Phillis Wheatley, an assimilationist like Benjamin Rush argued that she was intelligent only because she'd never really been a slave, i.e., slavery makes you dumb. News flash: Wheatley was intelligent because she had the opportunity to learn and wasn't tortured every day of her life. And even people who were tortured every day of their lives and did not have the opportunity to go to school still found ways to think and create. Still found ways to be human in their own way. Although their poetry looked different. Although they did not often have the opportunity to write their poetry.

See how that works, Mr. Rush? Mr. *Enlightened*? Huh? Yeah. Thanks, but no thanks.

While Rush was working to make this argument, Wheatley was over in London being trotted around like a superstar. The British would go on to publish her work. Not only would they publish her a year after slavery was abolished in England, they would use her (and Rush's pamphlet) as a way to condemn American slavery. Let me explain why that was a big deal. It's basically your mother telling you she's "not mad, but she's *disappointed* in you." Remember, America was made up of a bunch of Europeans, specifically British people. They still owned America. It was their home away from home (hence *New England*). The British disapproval applied pressure to the American slavery system, which was the American economic system, and in order for America to feel comfortable with continuing slavery, they had to get away from, break free of, Britain once and for all.

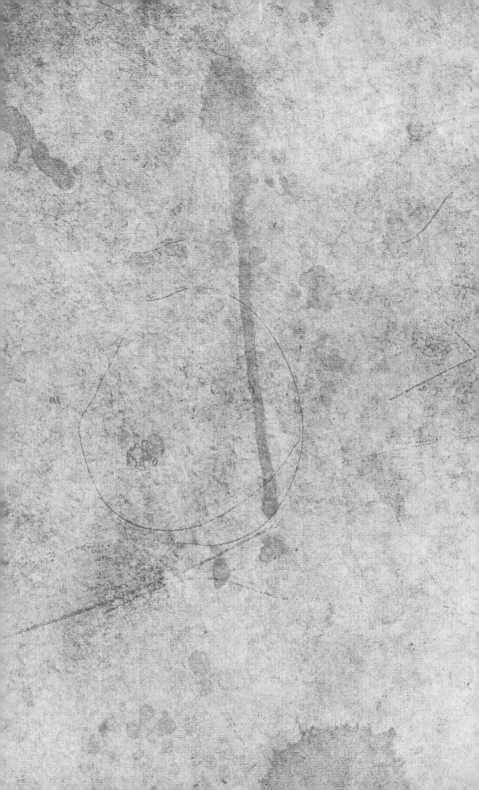

CHAPTER 6

Time Out

A QUICK RECAP OF RACIST IDEAS (SO FAR):

1. Africans are savages because Africa is hot, and extreme weather made them that way.

2. Africans are savages because they were cursed through Ham, in the Bible.

3. Africans are savages because they were created as an entirely different species.

4. Africans are savages because there is a natural human hierarchy and they are at the bottom.

5. Africans are savages because dark equals dumb and evil, and light equals smart and...White.

6. Africans are savages because slavery made them so.

7. Africans are savages.

Note: You will see these ideas repeated over and over again throughout this book. But that's not a good enough reason for you to stop reading. So...don't even try it.

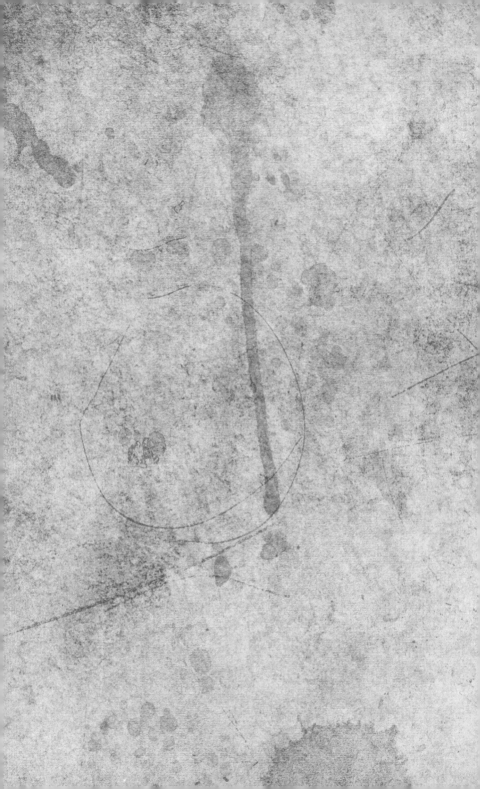

CHAPTER 7

Time In

AFRICANS ARE NOT SAVAGES.

CHAPTER 8

Jefferson's Notes

I KNOW YOU ALREADY KNOW THIS, BUT SOMETIMES IT'S important to put things in context so they really make sense.

Britain had ended slavery (at least in England, but not in the British colonies).

America refused to do so.

Britain looked at America as...dumb.

America said, "Mind your business, Britain."

Britain said, "You *are* my business, America."

America said, "Well, we can change that."

And in 1776, before anyone could spell W-E W-A-N-T S-L-A-V-E-R-Y, Thomas Jefferson, who at the time was a thirty-three-year-old delegate to the

Second Continental Congress, sat down to pen the Declaration of Independence. At the beginning of the declaration, he paraphrased the Virginia Constitution (every state has one) and wrote, "All men are created equal."

Bears repeating. All men are created equal.

Say it with me: All men are created equal.

But were slaves seen as "men"? And what about women? And what did it mean that Jefferson, a man who owned nearly two hundred slaves, was writing America's freedom document? Was he talking about an all-encompassing freedom or just America being free from England? While these questions hung in the air, slaves were taking matters into their own hands. They were running away from plantations all over the South by the tens of thousands. They wanted freedom, and guess who was to blame? Wait, first of all, guess who *should've* been blamed? Slaveholders, obviously. But Thomas Jefferson and other slave owners blamed Britain for inspiring this kind of rebellion. He'd written into the declaration all the ways Britain was abusing America, even stating that the British, though arguing against slavery, were actually trying to enslave (White) America. But remember, Jefferson agreed with slavery only as an economic system. I mean, he'd grown up with "Black friends," for goodness' sake. So, he also wrote into the declaration the antiracist sentiment that slavery was a "cruel war against human nature," but that part, and parts like it, were edited out by the other, more established delegates.

Over the next five years, the Americans and the British fought the Revolutionary War. And while British soldiers stormed the shores of Virginia looking for Jefferson, he was hiding out with his family, writing. Imagine that. The man who wrote the document that further fueled the war was hiding. As my mother says, "Don't throw a stone, then hide your hand." Jefferson was definitely hiding his hand. But he'd show it shortly after, because while hiding from capture, he decided to answer a series of questions, in writing, from a French diplomat who was basically collecting information about America (because America was becoming *AMERICA!*). And instead of just answering the questions, Jefferson decided to flex his muscle. To tell his truth.

He titled his book of answers *Notes on the State of Virginia*. In it, he expressed his real thoughts on Black people. Uh-oh. He said they could never assimilate because they were inferior by nature. Uh-oh. Said they felt love more, but pain less. Uh-oh. That they aren't reflective, and operate only on instincts. Yikes. That the freedom of slaves would result in the extermination of one of the races, i.e., a race war. *Uh-oh.* And the answer to "the problem" of slaves was that they should be sent back to Africa. So much for his "Black friends," huh? The ones he'd known to be intelligent blacksmiths, shoemakers, bricklayers, coopers, carpenters, engineers, manufacturers, artisans, musicians, farmers, midwives, physicians, overseers, house managers, cooks, and bi- and trilingual translators—all the workers who made his Virginia plantation and many others almost entirely self-sufficient.

Surprise, surprise.

Oh, the best part: He didn't intend to publish these notes widely, but a small devious printer did so without his permission.

Surprise, surprise!

When it came to Black people, Jefferson's whole life was one big contradiction, as if he were struggling with what he knew was true and what was *supposed* to be true. In 1784, Jefferson moved to Paris. His wife had died, and his old Monticello home suddenly felt pretty lonely. He was exhausted from his grief and years of being hunted by the British. So, he did what he always seemed to do in moments of crisis. He ran. To France. As soon as he made contact with the French foreign minister, he sent word home to his own slaves to speed up tobacco production in hopes that French merchants could pay back British creditors. On one hand, Jefferson was telling his slaves to work harder, and on the other hand he was telling abolitionists that there was nothing he wanted more than an end to slavery. And while he was busy playing the good guy, promoting, defending, and ensuring that the French knew America was becoming *AMERICA!* (and also having a good ol' French time), back home there was a convention taking place in Philadelphia to talk about the new constitution.

Turns out, Jefferson's declaration resulted in years of violent struggle with the British but, more important, it exposed a weak American government. So, this constitution was supposed to define it and solidify it. But before it was set in stone, there had to be a series of compromises.

1. **The Great Compromise:**
   This one created the House and the Senate. Two senators per state. House of Representatives based on population. The bigger the population, the more representatives each state could have to fight for its interests. This causes

issues, specifically between southern states and northern states, because they aren't sure how to count slaves. Which leads us to

2. The Three-Fifths Compromise:

The South wanted to play both sides of the fence. On one hand, they didn't want to count slaves as people, but instead wanted to count them as property, because the greater the population, the more taxes you have to pay. *But*, on the other hand, they needed more population, because the greater the population, the more representation they got, and with more representation came more power. And the North was like, "NOOOOPE! Slaves can't be human," because the North didn't have (as many) slaves and therefore couldn't risk letting the South have more power. So, the compromise was to create a fraction. Every five slaves equaled three humans. So, just to do the math, that's like saying if there were fifteen slaves in the room, on paper, they counted as only nine people.

This three-fifths-of-a-man equation worked for both the assimilationists and the segregationists, because it fit right into the argument that slaves were both human *and* subhuman, which they both agreed on. For the assimilationists, the three-fifths rule allowed them to argue that someday slaves might be able to achieve five-fifths. Wholeness. Whiteness. One day. And for segregationists, it proved that slaves were mathematically wretched. Segregationists and assimilationists may have had different intentions, but both of them agreed that Black people were inferior. And that agreement, that shared bond, allowed slavery and racist ideas to be permanently stamped into the founding document of America.

While all this was going on, Jefferson was in France, chillin'. That is, until the French Revolution broke out. At first, he didn't mind the French unrest. If anything, it made him happy to know America wasn't the only warring country. But then it spilled over into Haiti. And that was a problem. A *big* problem.

In August 1791, close to half a million enslaved Africans in Haiti rose up against French rule. It was a revolt like nothing anyone had ever seen. A revolt that the Africans in Haiti *won*. And because of that victory,

Haiti would become the Eastern Hemisphere's symbol of freedom. Not America. And what made that frightening to every American slaveholder, including Thomas Jefferson, was that they knew the Haitian Revolution would inspire their slaves to also fight back.

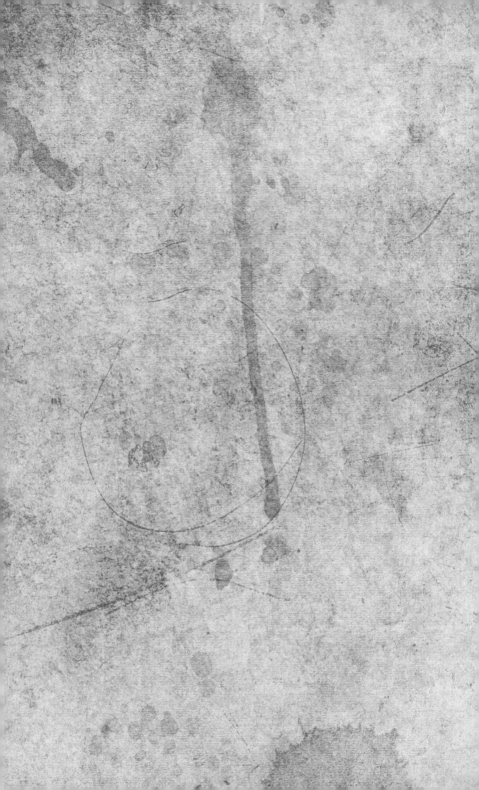

CHAPTER 9

Uplift Suasion

This is a short chapter.

Imagine it as a parenthetical, a side note, a *just so you know.*

Black people—slaves—started to get free. Runaways. And abolitionists urged the newly freed people to go to church regularly, learn to speak "proper" English, learn math, adopt trades, get married, stay away from vices (smoking and drinking), and basically live what they would consider to be respectable lives. Basically, live like White people. If Black people behaved "admirably," they could prove all the stereotypes about them were wrong.

This strategy was called uplift suasion. It was racist, because what it said was that Black people couldn't be accepted as themselves, and that they had to fit into some kind of White mold to deserve their freedom. But in the 1790s, uplift suasion was working. At least, it seemed to be.

It's important that you keep this in mind, because it would be the cornerstone of assimilationist thought, which basically said:

Make yourself small,

make yourself unthreatening,

make yourself the same,

make yourself safe,

make yourself quiet,

to make White people
comfortable with your
existence.

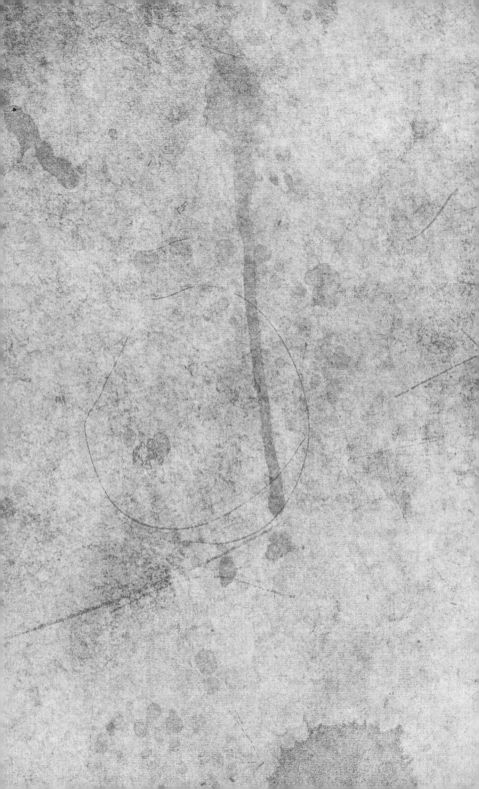

CHAPTER 10

The Great Contradictor

SCHOLAR. ASSIMILATIONIST. SLAVEHOLDER. MAN OF leisure. Author. Secretary of state. Vice president. But before Thomas Jefferson took on the role of president, his racist ideas took top position in the minds of many White people. Especially as slaves, many of whom were still inspired by the Haitian Revolution, were continuing to attempt insurrection.

Like Gabriel and Nancy Prosser. The Prossers were planning a slave rebellion, recruiting hundreds of slaves to revolt in Virginia. They had it all mapped out. And it was meant to be epic. Hundreds of captives were supposed to march on Richmond, where they would steal four thousand unguarded muskets, arrest the governor, and hold the city until other slaves arrived from surrounding counties to negotiate the end of slavery and the establishment of equal rights. Allies were to be recruited among Virginia's poor Whites and Native Americans. The lives of friendly Methodists, Quakers, and French people were to be spared. But racist Blacks, they would be killed. The Prossers took into account the fact that antiracists of any color were more necessary, more important to their liberation, than Black assimilationists. And this theory would be proved when the revolt—and their covers—were blown.

The revolt was scheduled for Saturday, August 30, 1800. But two cynical slaves—snitches—begging for their master's favor, betrayed what would have been the largest slave revolt in the history of North America, with as many as fifty thousand rebels joining in from as far away as Norfolk, Virginia. That was all it took for Governor James Monroe to have a militia waiting. Gabriel Prosser was eventually caught and hanged. Game over.

Well, not completely. More like, game changer.

The attempted (and failed) revolt made slave owners nervous. As it should've. So, up from the soil of slavery sprouted new racist ideas to protect White lives. Sending slaves "back" to Africa and the Caribbean—Thomas Jefferson's idea of colonization—was one of them.

Lots of people got behind the strategy of colonization, including (eventually) a delegate from Virginia, Charles Fenton Mercer, and an antislavery clergyman, Robert Finley. Finley would take the colonization idea and run with it. He started an organization called the American Colonization Society (ACS) and wrote the manifesto for it, outlining how free Blacks would need to be trained to take care of themselves so that they could go back to Africa and take care of their motherland. Build it up. Civilize it. But when all this was actually pitched to freed Black people, they weren't for it. Not having it. Black people didn't want to go "back" to a place they'd never known. They'd built America as slaves and wanted to reap the benefits of their labor as free people.

America was now their land.

This debate, the back-and-forth of what to do with slaves and free Blacks, was what Thomas Jefferson was stepping into when he became president in 1801. And his response to all the fuss was that he needed to put a policy in place that he thought might actually start the process of ending slavery, ultimately leading to colonization.

Wait. But he had slaves.

Wait. So, did he want to end slavery, but not free his own?

Wait. Was he proslavery *and* antislavery?

Contradiction. Could've been his middle name. Thomas *Contradiction* Jefferson. And that held true in 1807, when, as president, he brought about a new Slave Trade Act. The goal was to stop the import of people from Africa and the Caribbean into America, and fine illegal slave traders. (*Yes!*) Instead, the act turned out to be paper thin and did nothing to stop domestic slavery or the international slave trade. (*No!*) Kids were still being snatched from their parents, and slave ships were selling slaves "down river" from Virginia to New Orleans, which took just as many days as the trip across the Atlantic. (*Nooo!*) And Jefferson, the man who signed this Transatlantic Slave Trade Act, started "breeding" slaves. (*NO!*) He and other like-minded slave owners began forcing their men and women slaves to conceive children so that they, the owners, could keep up with all the farming demands of the Deep South. Slaves were being treated like human factories, birthing farming machines. Tractors with heartbeats. Backhoes that bleed.

CONTRADICTION.

But by the end of his presidential term, Jefferson had had enough. Of it all. For real this time. Done deal.

He was ready to step away from everything. From all the mess and madness of Washington and return to his home in Virginia, where he could read, write, and think. His *Notes on the State of Virginia* would've been a bestseller if bestsellers were a thing back then, and at this point in his life, he even wanted to be done with the fame it had brought him.

He seemed to be grinding a different gear now. At least, he was trying to. He'd apologized for slavery— P A U S E.

He'd apologized for slavery.

U N P A U S E. He'd retired and returned to Monticello, so he could…run his plantation— P A U S E.

So he could run his plantation?

U N P A U S E. He'd expressed remorse for slavery but still needed slave labor to pay his debts and pay for his luxuries. And on top of that, though he'd grown tired of the antislavery fight (which was also proslavery for him) he still, still, still continued to champion sending Black people back to Africa.

And if not Africa, Louisiana.

Jefferson had purchased the Louisiana Territory from the French early in his presidency. He'd wanted it to be the safe haven for freed slaves. It was supposed to be a bubble (pronounced *cage*) for Blacks, where they could be safe, and where White people could be safe from their potential response to, I don't know, the whole slavery thing. Colonization within the country, which was like Black people being banished to the basement of the house they'd built under the premise that it was better than sleeping in the street. But the Louisiana Territory got shaky when the question of Missouri came into play.

You have to remember that your map isn't the map they were using. The fifty states didn't exist yet. So, Louisiana, or as it was known then, the Louisiana Territory, took up the entire middle of the country. It stretched from north to south. It wasn't the "boot," as we know it now. Trombones and red beans? No.

The northern part of that swath of Louisiana was cut into what became the Missouri Territory. Its location— the Missouri part—was almost right smack in the middle of the country, meaning there was a geographical conundrum to be dealt with: Would Missouri be considered a slave state or a free state?

Well, the answer is, there was a bill passed to admit Missouri into the *Union* (the North) as a *slave* state. A man named James Tallmadge Jr. added an amendment to that bill that would've made it illegal for enslaved Africans to enter the new state, and stated that all children born from slaves *in* the state would be freed at the age of twenty-five. The Tallmadge Amendment sparked an explosive debate that burned for two years. Southerners saw this as a trick to limit the political power of southern agriculture and mess with their money and leverage in the House of Representatives, and therefore their power.

Ultimately, the debate was cooled by another compromise. The Missouri Compromise of 1820. Congress agreed to go on and admit Missouri as a slave state, but they'd also admit Maine as a free state to make sure there was still an equal amount of slave states and free states, so that no region, or way of governing, felt disadvantaged. Balance. And also to prohibit the introduction of slavery in the northern section of Jefferson's vast Louisiana Territory. His experimental land for colonization. An experiment that seemed unlikely.

But Jefferson would never give up on that idea. Even as he aged. And even though he didn't really support Finley's American Colonization Society, he still saw the mission as golden. He looked at it almost as if he'd be sending Black people home from camp, smarter and stronger and ready to build. Like it was benevolent and maybe even forgiving. Thomas *Contradiction* Jefferson, who grew up with *Black friends*, hoped it would all come out in the wash and that slavery would ultimately produce "more good than evil."

At least, that's one side of the coin. The smooth side. The textured side of Jefferson's intention was that he basically believed that sending Black people *back to where they came from* would make America what it was always meant to be in his eyes—a playground for rich White Christians. Despite the fact that Africans were brought to this land. Enslaved. Drained of their abilities and knowledge of growing and tending crops, exploited for their physical might and creativity when it came to building structures and making meals, stripped of their reproductive agency, stripped of their religions and languages, stripped of their dignity. American soil sopping with Black blood, their DNA now literally woven into the fibers of this land.

I wonder if Black people were thinking, *Where can we send you all? Back to Europe?* Or maybe instead of *sending* them, they were thinking more about *ending* them. It wouldn't be long before that choice was made for Jefferson.

By the spring of 1826, his health had deteriorated

to the point that he couldn't leave home. By summer, he couldn't even leave his bed, so sick he was unable to attend the fiftieth anniversary of the Declaration of Independence.

Aside from the children he had had with one of his slaves, Sally Hemings (how can you truly love humans you own?), Jefferson did not free any of the other enslaved people at Monticello, despite his believing that slavery was morally wrong, cementing once and for all the winner in his struggle between the ethical and the economic. One historian estimated that Jefferson had owned more than six hundred slaves over the course of his lifetime. In 1826, he held around two hundred people as property and he was about $100,000 in debt (about $2.5 million today), an amount so staggering that he knew that once he died, everything—and everyone—would be sold.

On July 2, 1826, Jefferson seemed to be fighting to stay alive. The eighty-three-year-old awoke before dawn on July 4 and called out for his house servants. The enslaved Black faces gathered around his bed. They were probably his final sight, and he gave them his final words. He had been a segregationist at times, an assimilationist at other times—usually both in the same act—but he never quite made it to being antiracist. He knew slavery was wrong, but not wrong enough to free his own slaves. He knew as a child that Black people were people, but never fully treated them as such. Saw them as "friends" but never *saw* them. He knew the freedom to live was fair, but not the freedom to live in America. The America built on their backs. He knew that *all men are created equal*. He wrote it. But couldn't rewrite his own racist ideas. And the irony in that is that now his life had come full circle. In his earliest childhood memory and in his final lucid moment, Thomas Jefferson lay there dying— death being the ultimate equalizer—in the comfort of slavery. Surrounded by a comfort those slaves never felt.

SECTION

3

1826 — 1879

CHAPTER 11

Mass Communication for Mass Emancipation

I HAD A FRIEND. LET'S CALL HIM MIKE. HE WAS SIX foot five and an easy three hundred pounds. A football player. I'd watched him truck people on the field, watched him put parents' children on gurneys all in the name of school pride and athletic victory. I'd watched him grunt and spit and slap himself around like a beast. And we cheered for him. Said his name on the morning announcements, wrote about him in the school paper, even held an in-school press conference when he committed to playing football in college.

But many of us cheered for him for other reasons. Because he also was part of the tap dance club. Because he played Santa Claus in the winter play. Because he took creative writing classes (with me) to explore his love of poetry. Because he spoke out against the mistreatment of young women in our school and stood up for classmates who were being bullied.

Mike didn't always get it right, but he was always open to learning and was never afraid to try.

The abolitionist William Lloyd Garrison was like that—a man with power and privilege, not afraid to try. But before we get to him, we have to address one of the greatest series of coincidences that led him to become a central figure in the conversation around race and abolitionism.

Coincidence 1:

Both Thomas Jefferson and John Adams (President #2, before Jefferson) died on July 4, 1826, on the fiftieth anniversary of the Declaration of Independence. Instead of people seeing this double death as a sign that the

old ways of doing things were out of style—
literally dead—people looked at their deaths
as some kind of encouragement to carry out
their legacies. It just so happens those legacies
were deeply entwined with slavery. Boston
had grown to nearly sixty thousand people
and was fully immersed in New England's
industrial revolution, which was now running
on the wheels of southern cotton.

Coincidence 2:
Though the revolutionary abolitionist movement was practically dead, Robert Finley's
American Colonization Society was still func-
tioning at full throttle, trying to get freed slaves
to go back to Africa and set up their own
colony. The ACS had asked a twenty-three-
year-old firebrand named William Lloyd
Garrison to give their Fourth of July address
in 1829. Garrison was the man. He was smart
and forward-thinking and worked as an editor
of a Quaker-run abolitionist newspaper. But
the ACS didn't know that Garrison had gone
even further to the side of abolitionism, *not*

colonization. He favored a gradual abolition—
a freedom in steps—but abolition nonetheless.
And that's what he spoke about at the ACS
conference, which, let's just say, was a little off
brand. Like someone speaking at a Nike conference, suggesting that the future of better
running wasn't better sneakers but better feet.
And Nike should figure out how to make better feet!

Garrison wasn't the only man who felt this way
(about abolishing slavery, not sneakers) and was unafraid
to speak out against colonization. David Walker was
another. Walker was a Black man, and he had written a
pamphlet, *An Appeal to the Coloured Citizens of the World*,
arguing against the idea that Black people were made
to serve White people. Walker's *Appeal* spread, Garrison
read it, and eventually the two men met. But before they
could really start making a mess of slavery, Walker, just
thirty-three years old, died of tuberculosis.

Garrison was influenced greatly by Walker's ideas and
carried them on, spreading them by doing what everyone
had done before him: Literature. Writing. Language.
The only difference was that Garrison's predecessors in

propaganda always spread damaging information. At least about Black people. They'd always printed poison, narratives about Black inferiority and White superiority. But Garrison would buck that trend and start a newspaper, the *Liberator*. The name alone was a match strike. This paper relaunched the abolitionist movement among White people. In his first editorial piece, Garrison changed perspectives from gradual abolition to immediate abolition. Meaning, he used to believe that freedom was incremental. A little bit at a time. A slow walk. Now he believed that freedom should be instant. Freedom right now. Immediately. Break the chains. Period. But (because there's always a *but*) immediate *equality*, well... that was a different story and, according to Garrison, should be... in steps. Gradual. So physical freedom now, but social freedom... *eventually*.

This idea of gradual equality was rooted in the same principles of uplift suasion. Blacks were seen as scary, and it was their responsibility to convince White people that they weren't. At least, this is what Garrison believed. But this idea was challenged by a man who disagreed with not only the idea of gradual equality but also the idea that Black people needed White people to save them, or that they—Black people—were part of the problem at all.

His name was Nat Turner. He was a slave and a preacher, and just as slave owners before the Enlightenment era believed slavery was a holy mission, Turner believed the same was true for freedom. That he was called upon by God to plan and execute a massive crusade, an uprising that would free slaves, and in so doing would leave slave masters, their wives, and even their children slaughtered. All in the name of liberation. And it did. There was a lot of bloodshed across the state of Virginia, until Turner finally got caught and hanged.

Again, slaveholders got scared. Tightened the yoke.

Garrison counteracted the intensity of the slave masters with an intensity of his own. He wrote a book that refuted colonizationists and gave birth to a new group called the American Anti-Slavery Society (AASS), a group of abolitionists. At the annual meeting of the AASS in May 1835, members decided to rely on the new technology of mass printing and an efficient postal service to overwhelm the nation with twenty to fifty thousand pamphlets a week. Garrison began flooding the market with new and improved abolitionist information. Social media before social media. And slaveholders had no clue what was coming: a million antislavery pamphlets distributed by the end of the year.

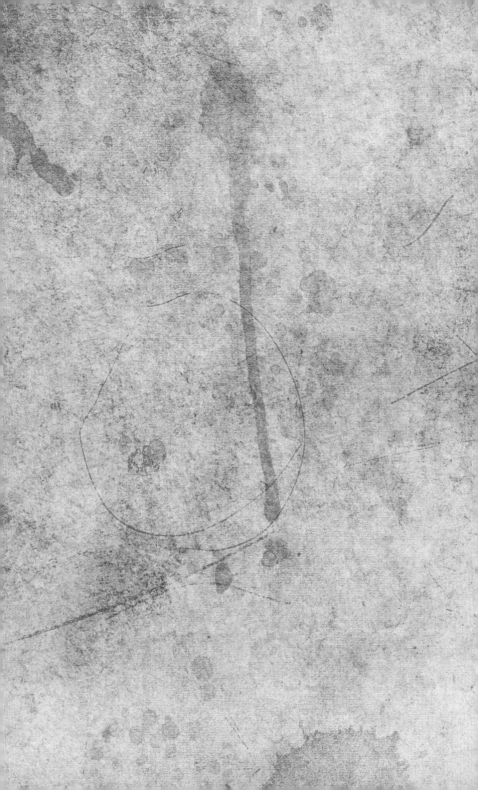

CHAPTER 12

Uncle Tom

WITH SO MUCH ANTISLAVERY INFO FLOATING AROUND, people—mainly White politicians and scholars—who were proslavery turned up the fear and hate, therefore turning up their ridiculous racist ideas. There were people still preaching that slavery was good, that it was the will of God. That equality between the races was impossible because the species were different. Yep, still stuck on the polygenesis theory, but this time it was backed by "science." There was a scientist, Samuel Morton, the father of American anthropology, who was measuring the skulls of humans (gross) and determined that White people had bigger skulls and therefore greater intellectual capacity, which, by the way, was how I combated being told all my life that I have a big head. *Yeah, because I got a big brain.* I never knew I was a scientist!

I also didn't know I was…insane. I'm not. But if I were alive and free back then, there's a good chance I would've been labeled as such. The US Census report of 1840 said that free Blacks were insane and enslaved Blacks were sane, and that biracial people had shorter life spans than Whites. Of course this wasn't true. They were cooking the books.

And, speaking of books, in Samuel Morton's *Crania Aegyptiaca*, he also introduced the narrative that historically there was a "White" Egypt that had Black slaves. Who knew? (The answer is no one. Not even Egyptians.) The propaganda just kept coming. Anything to justify supremacy and slavery.

And if bunk literature and false "studies" were the breakbeats of racism—looped samples pulsing on and on—then John C. Calhoun, a senator from South Carolina, was the emcee for slavery—an effective one—there to rock the racist crowd. Calhoun was fighting even for Texas to become a slave state in the 1844 election. He was running for office and angry that congressmen were even debating emancipation. Possibly ending slavery? An outrage! Calhoun eventually pulled out of the race, and it's a good thing he did, because William Lloyd Garrison was about to present a secret weapon to the abolitionist movement.

See, it's one thing to talk *around* slavery. To talk

about how the slaves lived, and what they were thinking, and how good they had it. It's another thing to hear a man who *was* a slave tell his own story. There was a new "special" Black person on the scene. A new Black exhibit. A new Phillis Wheatley, but this time not in need of a publisher. Garrison would be that.

That man's name was Frederick Douglass.

In June 1845, *The Narrative of the Life of Frederick Douglass, an American Slave* was published. It outlined Douglass's life and gave a firsthand account of the horrors of slavery. It was a hit, and a necessary weapon, to once again fight against the idea that Black people were subpar, and that White people were the benevolent Christians that the likes of Zurara and Cotton Mather worked so hard to portray. It was also meant to gain some kind of White sympathy. But Douglass was a runaway slave with a book about being a runaway slave, which meant he'd basically snitched on himself and needed to run farther away. So, he went to Great Britain and spread his antislavery message there, while in America proslavery politicians—now with Texas as a slave state—pushed for even more expansion, west.

Douglass's narrative wasn't the only one (is there ever only one?). In fact, the telling of his story sparked the telling of many others, including one about an enslaved woman—*The Narrative of Sojourner Truth*. Up until this point, women had been left out of the conversation around slavery. As if they weren't slaves. Or, as if they weren't slaveholders. Sojourner Truth was a former slave with the moxie of a woman slaveholder. The kind of woman who would stand up in a room full of White people and declare her humanity. She was bold, and that boldness, along with news about the Fugitive Slave Act, which was snatching free Blacks and sending them to the cotton fields, inspired a White writer to go on to write a book that would be much, much bigger than Truth's or Douglass's.

The book was called *Uncle Tom's Cabin*.

The author, Harriet Beecher Stowe.

NOTES ON *UNCLE TOM'S CABIN*:

1. Tom, a slave, is sold down the river.

2. He meets a young White girl, Eva.

3. Eva's father buys Tom.

4. Tom and Eva become friends,
   connecting over Christianity.

5. Eva dies two years later, but not before
   having a vision of heaven.

6. After her death, the White people
   decide to change their racist ways.

7. Eva's father even promises to free Tom.

8. Eva's father dies before he frees Tom,
   and Eva's mother sells Tom to a
   harsher slave owner.

9. This slave owner (Simon Legree)
   hates Tom for not whipping a fellow
   slave.

10. Legree tries to break Tom by breaking
    his faith. But Tom holds tight to
    Christianity. So, Legree has him
    killed.

Moral of the story: We all must be slaves...to God. And since docile Black people made the best slaves (to man), they made the best Christians. And since domineering Whites made the worst slaves, they made the worst Christians. So, slavery, though a brutal attack on Black humanity, was really just proof that White people were bad believers in Jesus.

I know. But, hey, it didn't have to make too much sense. Despite critiques by intellectual giants like William Lloyd Garrison, who pointed out in the *Liberator* the religious bigotry in the book and Stowe's endorsement of colonization, and by Frederick Douglass—from an assimilationist angle—who followed up by assuring Whites that the Black man, unlike the Native, *loves* civilization and therefore would never go back to Africa (as if Africa were uncivilized), *Uncle Tom's Cabin* exploded and became the biggest book of its time. Harriet Beecher Stowe became the J. K. Rowling of slave books. And even though Black men hated the novel because they were depicted as weak, Stowe's story was drawing more northerners to the abolitionist movement than the writings and speeches of Garrison and Douglass did in the 1850s. And that was no small feat. Garrison had used the *Liberator* as a consistent antiracist sounding board, and Douglass had boldly argued against polygenesis and proved there was no White Egypt, making him the world's most famous Black male abolitionist *and* assimilationist. But women were in support of Stowe. They were ready to fight for their rights and set the nation on fire.

Stowe was their gasoline.

And her novel was a time bomb that ticked and ticked and, after exploding, set the stage for a new political force, especially when it came to the conversation around slavery: Abraham Lincoln.

CHAPTER 13

Complicated Abe

WHEN WE THINK OF ABRAHAM LINCOLN, WE THINK Honest Abe, black suit, white shirt, top hat, beard. The Great Emancipator (hmmm), one of the best, or at least most, -known and -loved presidents in America's history.

That's what we're taught.

But Lincoln wasn't that simple. As I mentioned at the start of this journey, life rarely fits neatly into a box. People are complicated and selfish and contradictory. I mean, if there's anything we've learned from Thomas Jefferson, it's that you can be antislavery and not anti-racist. You cannot see Black people as people but know that mistreating and enslaving them are bad for business.

Bad for your brand. Bad for your opportunity. That's more in line of who Lincoln was.

Gasp. I know. This would mean we'd have to, perhaps, rethink the whole "Honest Abe" thing.

It wasn't that great a nickname anyway.

He wasn't even that great a politician, at first. Before he ever won, he lost. Got spanked in a Senate race in 1858 by a man named Stephen Douglas. Douglas was proslavery. Lincoln was fighting on behalf of the abolitionist movement—because you can't win if you don't have an opposing view to debate—and the Free Soilers, the people who believed slavery should not continue to extend west. The two men debated, and Douglas, slick tongued and sharp suited, wiped the racist floor with Lincoln and won the election.

But it wasn't a loss in vain. Though Lincoln was defeated, there was an obvious change in opinion in the country. A shift. Lincoln shifted with the shift and started to preach that slavery needed to end—but not because of the human horror. Because if labor was free, what exactly were poor White people expected to do to make money? If you weren't one of the wealthy White people who owned slaves, slavery didn't necessarily work in your favor. Lincoln was speaking out of... *three* sides of his mouth.

On one hand, he wanted slavery gone. Black people liked that. On another hand, he didn't think Black people should necessarily have equal rights. Racists loved that. And then, on a third hand (a foot, maybe?), he argued that the end of slavery would bolster the poor White economy, which poor White people loved. Lincoln had created an airtight case where no one could trust him (Garrison *definitely* didn't), but everyone kinda...wanted to. And when Lincoln lost, he'd still made a splash as his party, the Republican Party, won many of the House seats in the states that were antislavery. So much so, that Garrison, though critical of Lincoln, kept his critiques to himself because he saw a future where maybe—*maybe*—antislavery politicians could take over.

But it was politics as usual for Lincoln. Because he'd taken an antislavery approach against Stephen Douglas, the Republicans were labeled "Black Republicans," which was the worst thing to be called, obviously. There were still racists in the North. Still racists everywhere. And why would racists want to vote for the party "in support" of Black people? So, Lincoln changed his tune. Or maybe he just sang the *whole* song while running for president.

Lincoln was against Black voting.

Lincoln was against racial *equality*.

Lincoln and the party pledged *not* to challenge southern slavery.

And Lincoln won.

But with the sixteenth president of the United States in place, untrusting slaveholders broke into panic. Panic that the economic institution that kept them living like kings would be in jeopardy. Panic that they wouldn't be able to stop slave revolts and would be overthrown (Haiti! Haiti!). So, they did what most people, well… most bullies do when they've been bested on the playground. They—the South—took their ball and left.

The *secession*, which just means to withdraw from being a member of, not to be confused with *succession*, meaning a line of people sharing a role one after the other (like a succession of slave owners), not to be confused with *success*, which means to win (because that didn't happen), started with South Carolina. They left the Union. Which means they were starting their own territory, where they could make up their own rules and live their lives as racist as they wanted. Shortly thereafter, the rest of the South joined in on the disjoining. This was a big deal, because to lose an entire region meant the other states lost that region's resources. All that land. Those crops. Those people. That wealth. But it happened, and the split-offs called themselves the Confederacy. They voted in their own president, Jefferson Davis, who had declared that Black people should never and would never be equal to Whites. There were now two governments, like rival gangs. And what have gangs always done when one gang feels their turf is being threatened?

FIGHT!

Welcome to the Civil War.

The biggest change agent in the war was that slaves wanted to fight against their slave owners, and therefore join Northern soldiers in battle. They wanted the chance to fight against the thing that had been beating them, raping them, killing them. So, the first chance they got, they ran. They ran, ran, ran by the droves. They ran north to cross into the Union and join the Union army.

Anything for freedom.

And then got sent back.

Anything for slavery.

Union soldiers were enforcing the Fugitive Slave Act, which mandated that all runaways be returned to their owners. This was the summer of 1861. But by the summer of 1862, the slave act had been repealed and a bill passed that declared all Confederate-owned Africans who escaped to Union lines or who resided in territories occupied by the Union to be "forever free of their servitude." And it was this bill that would morph into an even bolder bill by Lincoln just five days later. "All persons held as slaves within any state [under rebel control] shall then, thenceforward, and forever, be free."

Just like that.

Lincoln was labeled the Great Emancipator, but really, Black people were emancipating themselves. By the end of 1863, four hundred thousand Black people had escaped their plantations and found Union lines. Meaning four hundred thousand Black people found freedom.

Or at least the potential for it. Because let's not pretend that life in the North, life across Union lines, was immediately sweet. It wasn't some bastion of peace and acceptance. The Union believed most of the same hype about Black people as the Confederacy. The only difference was they'd pushed past owning them a little sooner. But their feelings toward Black people—that they were lazy and savage and blah, blah, blah—were the same. On top of that, there were many Black people who feared that freedom would be nothing without land. What good was it to be free if they had nowhere to go and no way to build a life for themselves? And what about voting? These were a couple of the questions at hand, a few of the issues Lincoln was trying to work through. What he *was* comfortable with, however, was the way Black people praised him. They'd run up to him in the street, drop to their knees, and kiss his hands. And when the Civil War finally ended in April 1865, on the eleventh day of that same month, Lincoln delivered his plans for reconstruction. And in that plan, he said what no president had ever said before him—that Blacks (the intelligent ones) should have the right to vote.

No wonder three days later he was shot in the back of the head.

CHAPTER 14

Garrison's Last Stand

As QUICKLY AS THINGS ARE DONE, THEY ARE ALSO UNDONE.
Three weeks after Lincoln's death, William Lloyd
Garrison, who had been steady on his antiracist journey—
producing antiracist literature in the *Liberator*, including
his critiques of Lincoln's racist political ploys, and his
work for the American Anti-Slavery Society—called it
quits. He announced his retirement. He believed that
because emancipation was imminent, his job as an abolitionist was done. But his team, his followers, refused
to stop their work, and instead shifted their focus to
Black voting. A focus that leaned toward immediate
equality. And while Garrison was trying to bow out

gracefully, Lincoln's successor was forcefully breaking in. And breaking down what had been, for Black people, a breakthrough.

His name was Andrew Johnson, and he basically reversed a lot of Lincoln's promises, allowing Confederate states to bar Blacks from voting, and making sure their emancipation was upheld only if Black people didn't break laws. Black codes—social codes used to stop Black people from living freely—were created. They would quickly evolve into Jim Crow laws, which were laws that legalized racial segregation. No need for the loopholes anymore. All this was under President Johnson's watch. He emboldened the Ku Klux Klan, allowing them to wreck Black lives with no consequence and enshrine those racist codes and laws. Turned out, freedom in America was like quicksand. It looked solid until a Black person tried to stand on it. Then it became clear that it was a sinkhole.

Antiracists were fighting against all these things. Some people, like Pennsylvania congressman Thaddeus Stevens, even fought for the redistribution of land to award former slaves forty acres to work for themselves. But the arguments against this plan were relentless and racist, presented in this strange way that makes the freed

Black person seem stupid. *How will they know how to care for the land if it's just given to them?* Um... really?

And guess who was quiet? William Lloyd Garrison. Having suffered two bad falls in 1866 that physically sidelined him, he chose not to engage in the political struggle against racial discrimination. But he still looked on, watching the racist roadblocks being erected at every turn, and the political and physical violence working to break the bones of Black liberation. Yes, Garrison still looked on, his ideas about gradual equality still evolving. After all, it had been his genius, whether he knew it or not, that had transformed abolitionism from a messy political stance (like Jefferson's) to a simple moral stance: Slavery was evil, and those racists justifying or ignoring slavery were evil, and it was the moral duty of the United States to eliminate the evil of slavery.

Boom.

Andrew Johnson was one of the evil. He did everything he could to keep Black people as "free" slaves. In response, Black people had to fight to build their own institutions. Their own spaces to thrive, like colleges, or as they're now called, Historically Black Colleges and Universities (HBCUs). From there came the Black (male) politician. And eventually, on February 3,

1870, the Fifteenth Amendment was made official. The amendment made it so that no one could be prohibited from voting due to "race, color, or previous condition of servitude." But the thing about this amendment (as well as the Thirteenth and Fourteenth) was that there were loopholes. Racist loopholes. *Potholes.* See, the amendment doesn't state that Black politicians would be protected. Or that the voting requirements would be equal.

Even so, racists didn't want the amendment to be pushed through because they saw giving the right to vote to all Black people as the establishment of some kind of Black supremacy. Really, it was just Black equality. Black opportunity. Black people from Boston to Richmond to Vicksburg, Mississippi, planned grand celebrations after the ratification. For their keynote speaker, several communities invited a living legend back to the main stage. William Lloyd Garrison.

The Fifteenth Amendment was a big deal. But here's the thing about big deals. If people aren't careful, they can be tricked into believing a big deal is a done deal. Like there's no more fight left. No reason to keep pushing. That freedom is an actual destination. And that's how Garrison and the American Anti-Slavery Society felt. Like their jobs were done. They disbanded in 1870.

Everyone let their guard down, and the racists were right there with right hooks and uppercuts to the face of freedom.

Bring on the White terrorism.

Bring on more propaganda about brute and savage Blacks.

Bring on Black people doing their best to fight back.

BLACK EMPOWERMENT.

Bring on women fighting back.

WOMEN EMPOWERMENT.

Bring on political pacifiers.

Bring on more talks about colonization, this time to the Dominican Republic.

Bring on domestic migration. To Kansas. Freedom from a second slavery.

It was this, Black people moving to safer pastures like Kansas, that William Lloyd Garrison supported at the end of his life. With Black people eager to leave the South, eager to give themselves a chance at safety, Kansas seemed to make more sense than the ever-present conversation of colonization to Africa. Or even the North. Or the far West. Northern allies worked tirelessly to raise money for southern Black people who wanted to flee Mississippi or Louisiana. Garrison, now seventy-four, his abolitionist heart still pumping, exhausted himself gathering resources for hundreds of Black people on the move toward Kansas.

It was the best he could do.

He'd wanted immediate emancipation. He now even wanted immediate equality. Neither of those things happened during the Reconstruction after the Civil War. And neither of them would in his lifetime.

SECTION 4

1868 – 1963

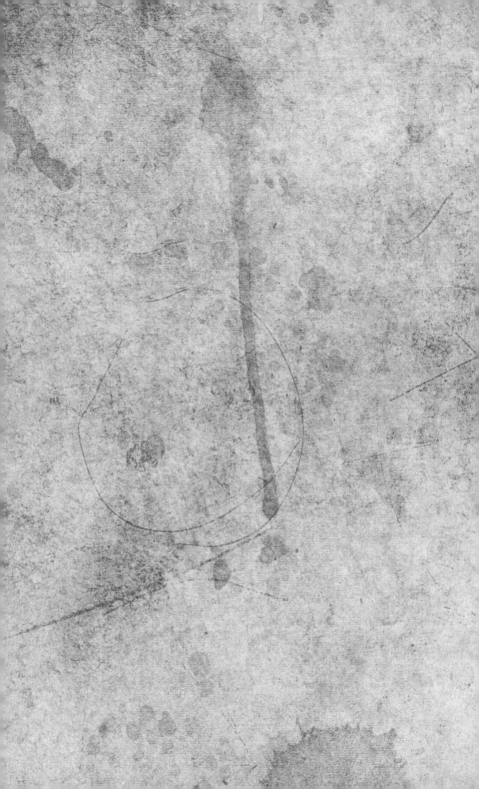

CHAPTER 15

Battle of the Black Brains

THIS IS A REMINDER.

This is not a history book. But there are some names in this story that you've read in history books. Names you know. At least names you should know. It's okay if you don't know them, because that's what this *not history* history book is for. But...I'm sure you know this one, because his name *definitely* comes up every February.

William Edward Burghardt Du Bois, or as he was known when he was younger, Willie Du Bois, or as he was known when he was older, W. E. B. Du Bois, because nicknames are awesome when you have four names. He and his brother were raised in Massachusetts, by a single mother who struggled to take care of them. Young

Willie was hit with his first racial experience on an inter-racial playground when he was ten years old, in the same way many of us experience our first racial experiences. A girl refused a card from him. Okay, maybe this isn't the first *racial* experience for a lot of us, but a lot of us have experienced, and will experience, this kind of rejection. Some of us will experience it romantically—she/he/they just aren't that into you—and others of us, like Du Bois, will experience it as a direct result of our differences. In his case, his biggest difference was the color of his skin. That's all he needed to begin competing with his White classmates, determined to convince them that he was not different. And if he was different, it was because he was better.

W. E. B. Du Bois didn't know it at ten years old, but he was going to become the king of uplift suasion. The king of *I can do anything they can do.* The king of *If I'm like you, will you love me?* Making him, without a doubt, the Black king of assimilation.

At least for a while.

But we'll get to all that.

For now, let's get into how Du Bois as a teenager decided, like Phillis Wheatley a few generations before him, that he wanted to go to Harvard. All-White

Harvard. But, of course, that wasn't an option. So, the townspeople—good White folks—pooled their money and sent young Willie to Fisk University, in Nashville, the best Black school in the country and the top of the top when it came to teaching Black people uplift suasion. Du Bois gobbled up the lessons on how to win White people over. And after his time at Fisk, Du Bois was able to put what he'd learned about assimilationism into practice.

His dream had come true. He got into Harvard to earn a postgraduate degree.

But not only did he get in, he did so well there that he even spoke at his graduation.

W. E. B. Du Bois had graduated from the best Black school and the best White school, proving the capabilities of Black people. At least in his own mind. Like I said, he was obsessed with keeping up with White people. Running their race. But in his speech, he gave credit to Jefferson Davis—Jefferson Davis!—saying that the Confederate president represented some kind of rugged individualism, as opposed to the "submissive" nature of the slave. Yikes. Just as John Cotton and Richard Mather had planned several generations before, these ideas were coming out of Du Bois's Ivy League classrooms, where he'd basically been fed the same narrative that Black people had been ruined by slavery. That they were irredeemable, in desperate need of fixing but unfortunately unfixable, which meant he was obviously exceptional, and…an exception. But the root of his exceptionalism, his excellence, came from his being biracial. It *must* have. According to one of Du Bois's intellectual mentors, mulattoes were practically the same as any White man.

Du Bois even went so far as to blame Black people for being mistreated. Blamed them for fighting back, which meant he blamed them for being lynched. For instance, when White people challenged the Fifteenth Amendment—the right to vote—by attaching an educational qualification to what was supposed be a freedom for *all*, Du Bois, an educated man, found fault in the Black rage. And found justification in the White response to the Black rage. Because Black people were breaking the law by wanting White people to stop breaking the law. That they were wrong for wanting to live. And Du Bois wasn't the only Black man who believed that Black men were bad. Booker T. Washington, the shining star of Tuskegee Institute—a college that cranked out Black brilliance—believed this, and even a dying Frederick

Douglass did. As a matter of fact, it took a young anti-racist Black woman to set these racist men straight.

Ida B. Wells-Barnett was an investigative journalist who did the necessary research to expose the inconsistencies in the data. In a pamphlet she published in 1892 called *Southern Horrors: Lynch Law in All Its Phases*, she found that from a sampling of 728 lynching reports, only a third of Black men lynched had actually "ever been *charged* with rape, to say nothing of those who were innocent of the charge." White men were lying about Black-on-White rape and hiding their own assaults of Black women. But the accusation of rape could make it easier for southern White men to puff up and act maliciously, all in the name of defending the honor of White women. And Du Bois didn't challenge it.

Do the crime, do the time.

Don't do the crime...die.

I know. W. E. B. Du Bois doesn't really sound that awesome. So, let's talk about someone else.

Booker T. Washington. (Strike that thing I just said about him a few lines up. Actually, don't strike it, because it's true. But...there's more.)

Booker T. Washington wanted Blacks to focus on what would now be called blue-collar work. While Du Bois was rubbing elbows in the halls of the White academy, Washington was in the fields. Well, not really. Though he was the head of Tuskegee, his push for civil rights was more of a backdoor approach. After Frederick Douglass's death in 1895, Washington stepped into his place as the new leader of Black America, and though *privately* he supported empowerment, what he advised was that Black people *publicly* focus on lower pursuits, such as tending the fields. Labor. Common work. Because he knew that would be more acceptable to White people. Knew they would eat it up. Why wouldn't they? A Black man saying, post-slavery, that Black people should be happy with the bottom, because at least the bottom is a dignified start. For White people, that sounded perfect, because it meant there was a greater chance Black people would stay out of positions of power, and therefore would never actually have any.

Oof. I guess Booker T. Washington really doesn't sound that great, either.

Du Bois believed in being like White people to eliminate threat so that Black people could compete. Washington believed in eliminating thoughts of competition so that White people wouldn't be threatened by Black sustainability. And there were Black people who believed both men, because, though we're critiquing their assimilationist ideas in this moment, they were thought leaders of their time. The wildest part about these two men is that they didn't get along. They were like the Biggie and Tupac of their day. Or maybe Michael Jackson and Prince. Hmm, maybe Malcolm and Martin. They believed in the destination, which was Black freedom, but, regarding the journey there, they couldn't have disagreed more.

Du Bois, the hyper-intellectual golden child. Washington, the man of the people.

Du Bois wrote *The Souls of Black Folk*, which intellectualized who Black people really were. Washington wrote *Up from Slavery*, which outlined the diligence, faith, and fortitude it took (and takes) to survive in America, coupled with the idea of the "White savior."

Stories featuring White people having antiracist epiphanies or moments of empathy resulting in the "saving" of Black people—White savior stories—were becoming a fixture in American media, and the problem with them wasn't that there weren't any "good" White people in real life, it's that the stories gave the illusion that there were more than there really were. That White people, in general, were (once again) the "saviors" of Black people.

Because of that (partially), *Up from Slavery* was a hit. And Du Bois couldn't take it. He couldn't stomach the fact that Washington was in the spotlight, shining. Washington was even invited to the White House once Theodore Roosevelt got into office, while the always sophisticated Du Bois publicly critiqued Washington, calling him old-fashioned for being so accommodating to White people, for presenting the idea that Black people should find dignity through work, and that no education was complete without the learning of a trade. Meanwhile, his own book, *The Souls of Black Folk*, set out to establish the mere fact that Black people were complex human beings. It was in this work that Du Bois introduced the idea of double consciousness. A two-ness. A self that is Black and a self that is American. And from this he fashioned a sample set of Black people who sat at the converging point. Black people to be "positive" representatives of the race. Like, if Blackness—"good" Blackness—was a brand, Du Bois wanted *these* Black people to be the ambassadors of that brand. One in every ten, he believed, were worthy of the job. He called them the Talented Tenth.

Though Du Bois was against accommodating White people—at least, that's what he criticized Washington for—he was still the same man fighting for White approval. He still believed that he could think and dress and speak racism away. No matter what he said about Washington's antics and "accommodation," W. E. B. Du Bois was, in fact, still the emperor of uplift suasion.

But Du Bois would get a wake-up call. A slap in the face, even. Not from Washington, but from a man named Franz Boas, who had immigrated to America from Germany in 1886 because of anti-Jewish persecution. Boas had become one of America's most prominent anthropologists and had been drawing similarities between the way his people were mistreated in Germany and the way Black people were being mistreated in America—with each nation justifying the treatment by saying the persecuted group was naturally inferior. Same story, different book. But in 1906, when Du Bois asked Boas to come speak at Atlanta University (where he was teaching), he had no idea what he was in for. Boas affirmed that the idea that Black people are naturally inferior, or even that they've been made inferior from slavery, was false, and all one needed to do to prove this was dig through the history of Black people *before* they got to America. Black people had a history. And that history—an African history—wasn't one of inferiority. Instead, it was one full of glorious empires, like those of Ghana, Mali, and Songhay, full of intellects and innovators.

Du Bois's head blew right off his shoulders. At least, that's the way I imagine it. Either way, his mind and all the White mumbo jumbo he'd consumed had started to change.

But the intellectual high wouldn't last, because by the end of that same year, Black people helped the Republicans regain the House of Representatives in the midterm elections, and as soon as they did, Roosevelt, the president who'd invited Booker T. Washington to his house—the most popular president among Black people ever—kicked a bunch of Black soldiers out of the army. Without any money. One hundred sixty-seven soldiers, to be exact. A dozen of them had been falsely accused of murdering a bartender and wounding a cop in Texas. These soldiers, of the 25th Infantry Regiment, were a point of pride for Black America. For them to be mistreated, as fighters for a country that had been fighting against them their entire lives, was a blow to the Black psyche. And just like that, Roosevelt was seen as a back-stabber by Black people. And because Booker T. Washington was Roosevelt's guy, his man, his "Black friend," Washington also had to feel the wrath when the president hurt his people.

Due to the social blow Booker T. Washington took because of his familiar and "friendly" history with Roosevelt, Du Bois's Talented Tenth rose in influence.

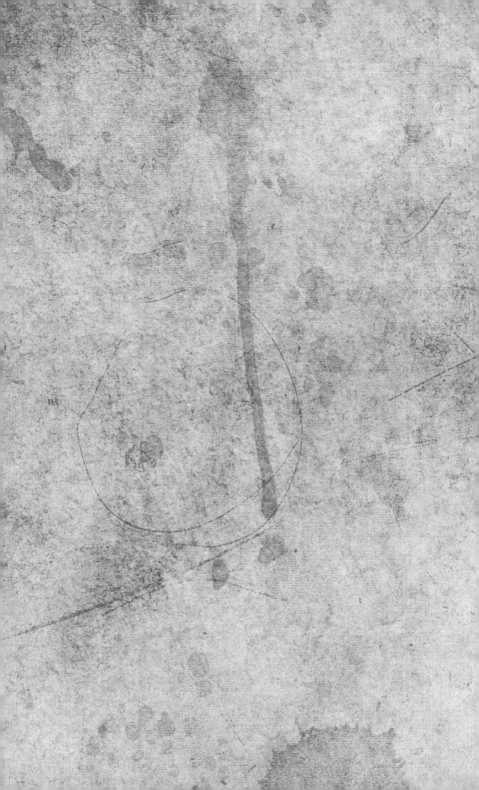

CHAPTER 16

Jack Johnson vs. Tarzan

THE FIGHTING BETWEEN DU BOIS AND WASHINGTON was nothing compared with the actual boxing that gripped the entire nation. Black people used Black fighters as a way to symbolically beat on White America's racism. White people used White fighters to prove superiority over Black people in the ring, and therefore in the world. No boxer broke the backs of White people, and puffed up the chests of Black people, like Jack Johnson.

He was the most famous Black man in America. And the most hated. Because he was the best. He'd beaten the brakes off every White boxer, and in December 1908, he finally got a shot at the heavyweight title. His opponent, Tommy Burns. The fight took place in Australia, and, well, let's just say Jack left Tommy "down under." I know, a bad joke. A dad joke. A bad dad joke. But still, a fact.

For racists, athletes and entertainers could be spun into narratives of the Black aggressor, the natural dancer, etc. Like, the reason Black people were good wasn't because of practice and hard work but because they were born with it. (Note: Black assimilationists have also made this argument.) Which is racist. It gave White people a way to explain away their own failures. Their competitive losses. Also gave them justification to find ways to cheat, inside the arena or outside.

For Black people, however, sports and entertainment were, and still are, a way to step into the shoes of the big-timer. It was a way to use the athlete or the entertainer—Johnson being both—as an avatar. As a representative of the entire race. Like human teleportation machines, zapping Black people, especially poor Black people, from powerlessness to possibility. So, if Johnson arrived on the scene dressed in fancy clothes, hands adorned with diamonds, all Black people were psychologically dressed to the nines. At least for a while. If Johnson talked slick to White men, saying whatever he wanted, all Black people got away with a verbal jab or two (in their minds). And, most important, if Johnson knocked out a White man, guess what? All Black people knocked out a White man.

And White people couldn't have that.

Immediately, White people started to cry out for a "Great White Hope" to beat Johnson. That "hope" was a retired heavyweight champion, James J. Jeffries. Retired. Their hope was someone who had already quit the sport. Really. I mean... *come on.*

No need to build suspense. You know what happened.

Jeffries lost, too, and though this was a big deal, especially for White people, it was everything else about Jack Johnson—not just his fighting—that set off alarms in the racist world.

1. His ego. Jack Johnson was a champ
    who acted like a champ. Fur coats
    and diamonds. An early god of flash.
    And...

2. The biggest spike in the heart of
    White America: Jack Johnson's wife...
    was white. (Cue the dramatic organ or
    the gunshots or the thunder crack or
    the hissing cat or...)

Johnson had too much power. Power to defeat White men. Power to be with White women. And, just like with the Haitian Revolution, White people were afraid all Black men would feel just as powerful, and that was a no-go. So, they figured out a way to get rid of Jack Johnson. To stop him. They arrested him on trumped-up charges for trafficking a prostitute (or rather a White woman) across state lines. He ran, spent seven years out of the country before turning himself in and doing a year in jail.

But the end of Jack Johnson still wasn't enough to make White men feel good about themselves, so a man named Edgar Rice Burroughs wrote a book to reinforce the idea of White supremacy and to remind White men that Africans (Black people) were savages. It was called *Tarzan of the Apes*.

Here's the basic plot of the book series:

1. A White child named John Clayton is orphaned in central Africa.

2. John is raised by apes.

3. They change his name to Tarzan, which means "white skin."

4. Tarzan becomes the best hunter and warrior. Better than all the Africans.

5. Eventually he teaches himself to read.

6. In the sequels and subsequent stories, Tarzan protects a White woman named Jane from being ravished by Africans.

7. Tarzan protects a White woman named Jane from being ravished by Africans.

8. Tarzan protects a White woman named Jane from being ravished by Africans.

9. Get it?

Tarzan was bigger than Jack Johnson ever was or would be. He became a cultural phenomenon, made into comic strips, movies, television shows, and even toys. I'm sure some of you have seen the movies or the old TV shows, in which Tarzan does that yodel, a call of White masculinity that we've all mimicked as children. At least I did.

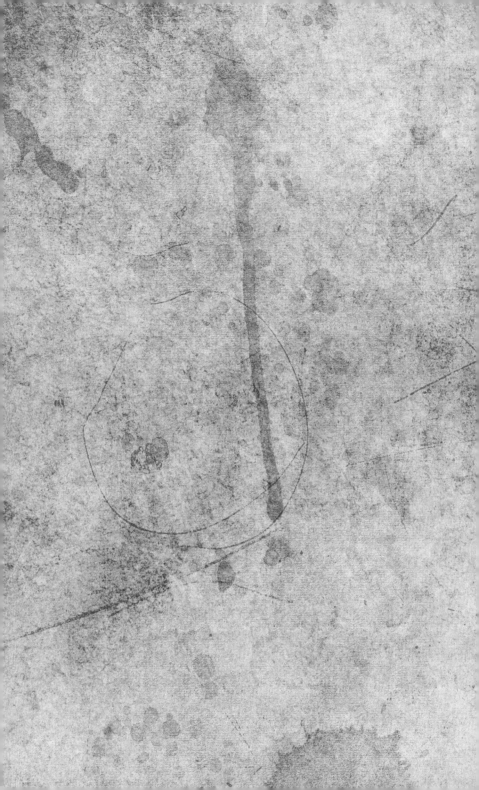

CHAPTER 17

Birth of a Nation (and a New Nuisance)

THE SAME YEAR THE FIRST TARZAN NOVEL WAS PUB-lished, Black people got tricked again (AGAIN) by a political candidate. They helped to get the Democrat Woodrow Wilson elected.

Now seems like a good time to address the whole Republican/Democrat thing. At this point in history, the Democrats dominated the South. They were opposed to the expansion of civil rights and anything that had to do with far-reaching federal power, like railroads, settling the West with homesteaders and not slave owners, even state university systems. Today, we'd say they were against "Big Government." Republicans at this time dominated the North. They were "for" civil rights (at least politically) and wanted expansion and railroads, and even a state university system.

I know. It feels like I got their descriptions mixed up. Like we're living in backward land. Maybe we are.

Anyway, back to Woodrow Wilson. He was a Democrat. And during his first term, he let Black people know what he thought about them by enjoying the first-ever film screening in the White House, of Hollywood's first blockbuster film, D. W. Griffith's *The Birth of a Nation*. The film was based on a book called *The Clansman*. Can you guess what this movie was about?

Here's the basic plot:

1. A Black man (played by a White man in blackface) tries to rape a White woman.

2. She jumps off a cliff and kills herself.

3. Klansmen avenge her death.

4. The end.

The beginning of a new outrage. I want to be clear here.

Rape isn't something to be taken lightly or to be turned back on the victim as a sharp blade of blame. But during this time, allegations of rape were often used as an excuse to lynch Black men, rooted in the stereotype of the savagery of the Black man and the preciousness of the White woman. Black people protested the movie. The intellects, like Booker T. Washington and W. E. B. Du Bois, fought in their intellectual ways. Writing. But southern Black activists did much more. They protested with their feet.

It was time to go.

It's important to note that this was during the Great War, also known as World War I, but the great war at home between Blacks and Whites had pushed Blacks to the brink. Black people started to leave the South in droves. Imagine the biggest parade you've ever seen, and then multiply it by a bazillion, but it didn't look as uniform or as happy. This was a parade of progress. One of hope after severe exhaustion. Black people were tired of being lied to. Tired of being told life was better after emancipation, as if Jim Crow laws hadn't made their lives miserable. As if politicians hadn't taken advantage of them, milking them for votes to gain power, only to slap Black people back down. As if the media hadn't continued to push racist narratives that would put Black people's lives at risk, off page and off screen.

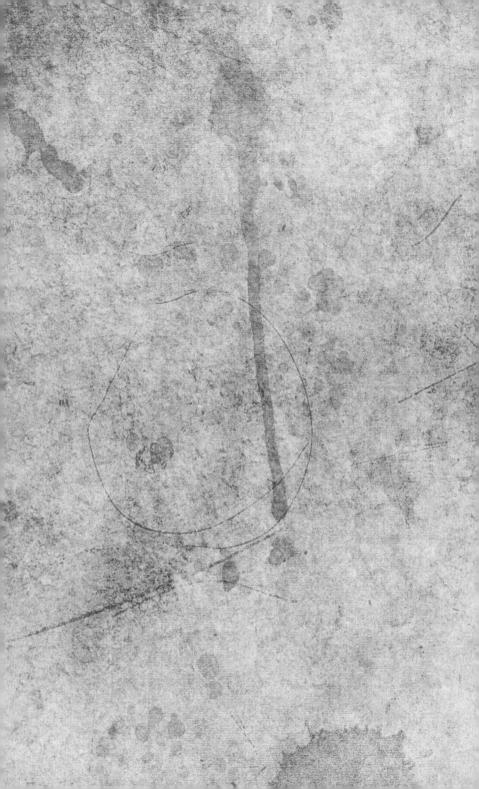

CHAPTER 18

The Mission Is
in the Name

BLACK PEOPLE FROM THE SOUTH WERE HEADED TO Chicago. To Detroit. To New York. Some even came from the Caribbean to escape colonialism. A Jamaican man, Marcus Garvey, was one of them. He'd come to America to raise money for a school in Jamaica, and the first thing he did once he arrived in New York in 1916 was visit the NAACP office.

The NAACP was started by two men who had written books about the antislavery activist John Brown. In 1859, Brown—a White man—raided the United States Armory in Harpers Ferry, West Virginia, with the intention of arming slaves and starting a revolution. He was caught and, of course, executed. Du Bois wrote Brown's biography, and the year it was published, 1909, was also the year a man named Oswald Garrison Villard published his biography of John Brown. Villard was White and happened to be William Lloyd Garrison's grandson. Who do you think sold more books? But instead of Du Bois cutting Villard down like he did Booker T. Washington, he decided to work with Villard to form the National Association for the Advancement of Colored People (NAACP). Their mission was in the name.

And when Marcus Garvey showed up, he was expecting that mission to be shown in the actual people working for the organization. See, Garvey was looking for Du Bois, but when he got to the office, he was confused about whether the NAACP was a Black organization or a White one. And that was simply because no one dark-skinned worked there. It was as if the only Black people who could succeed in America were biracial or lighter skinned. As if the Talented Tenth were the only Black people of value. Such an assimilationist way of thinking. An antiracist like Garvey saw all Black people as valuable. Saw Blackness as valuable, in culture and in color. So Garvey decided to set up shop in Harlem and start his own organization, called the Universal Negro Improvement Association (UNIA). Its purpose was to focus on African solidarity, the beauty of dark skin and African American culture, and global African self-determination. He basically created the exact opposite of the Talented Tenth.

Garvey wasn't the only one who noticed the growing power of biracial Americans. Scholars were paying attention. Eugenicists—people who believed you could control the "quality" of human beings by keeping undesirable genetics out, meaning the genetics of Black people—were criticizing and berating the mixing of races, because Whiteness was seen as pure. There were new versions of the racial hierarchy, which weren't that new because Black people still existed at the bottom, but the argument was that the more White (Nordic) blood people had, the better they would be, intellectually. Listen, I could give you more of their lines, but I've said this a million times by now. They were arguing what they'd been arguing—that Black people were born to be less-than, and that mixing with Whites gave them a leg up because they then weren't "all the way" Black. This would tie in with the creation of IQ tests and standardized tests, all skewed to justify the dumb Black, and the ones that did well *must've* had some White in them. Yada yada yada.

Yet in the midst of the Great War, Black men were good enough to fight. Smart enough to be tactical. Motivated enough to run, roll, shoot, and save. Of course.

Du Bois went over to Paris after the war ended to document the stories of Black soldiers for the *Crisis*, the newspaper he'd started. The stories he was told, and that he documented, were ones of Black heroes. But when the White officers came back to the States to tell their versions of the stories, the Black heroes had become Black nothings. More important, Black soldiers had been treated relatively well in France. And the president at the time, Woodrow Wilson, feared that being treated decently overseas would embolden Black soldiers. Make them too big for their britches. Make them expect fair treatment at home, the home for which they'd just risked their lives.

Let that sink in.

The home for which they bled for. Killed for. This was the final gust of wind (not really the final, but he was getting there) on Du Bois's tiptoe tightrope walk of racism. His past critiques of antiracists, spinning them into imaginary hate-mongers, had finally come back to bite him. He'd spent so many years trying to convince

Black people to mold themselves into a version of White people. He'd spent so much time trying to learn, speak, dress, and impress racism away. He'd tried to provide White Americans with the scientific facts of racial disparities, believing reason could kill racism, as if reason had birthed it. He had even spent energy ridiculing leaders like Ida B. Wells-Barnett for passionately calling on Black people to fight. But every year, as the failures for freedom piled up, Du Bois's urgings for Black people to protest and fight became stronger.

Du Bois, the king of assimilation, began calling out White men's twisting of words. It was time for a *New* Negro, he preached. One that would no longer sit quietly, waiting to assimilate. And in 1919, when many of those soldiers came home from war, they came home as New Negroes.

Unfortunately, New Negroes were met by Old Whites. Violence. The normal racist ideas weren't working on Black people, so racists had to go above and beyond. The summer of 1919 was the bloodiest summer since Reconstruction. So much so, it was named Red Summer. Du Bois responded to Red Summer with a collection of essays arguing many things about Black people being people, but one of the most revolutionary things he did in the collection was honor Black women. This was a huge deal, because Black women had either been completely left out of the race conversation or turned into objects to look at and take advantage of.

Even though Du Bois had done this, Marcus Garvey, the Jamaican who had taken issue with the NAACP, still despised him. Like I said, Garvey was a staunch antiracist; though Du Bois was making antiracist strides, he was still straddling the assimilationist line, and Garvey thought he was condescending to his own race. That he moved and acted like he was a better Black person. A special Black person. An exception. And, of course, there was the biggest beef of all, the conflict around the premise that lighter-skinned people were being given advantages and treated better—colorism. Garvey wasn't completely wrong. Though Du Bois wanted Black people to be a people with the freedom to be different when it came to art and music and spirituality, he definitely looked at himself as the standard. So, if you weren't him—light-skinned, hyper-educated—you weren't quite good enough. He also reinforced Harriet Beecher Stowe's idea that Black people had more soul than Whites (which meant they had less mind) and therefore were better at creative things. Garvey would've argued against that, but he didn't get the chance to, because the US government charged him with mail fraud, and he was deported three years later.

With no one there to challenge him, Du Bois's old crutch that he just couldn't seem to divorce himself from, uplift suasion, was about to transform into a different kind of *be my friend* bait.

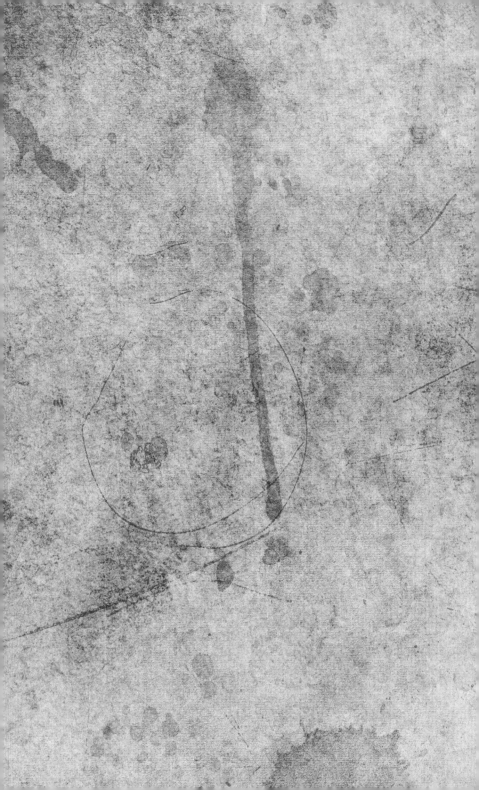

CHAPTER 19

Can't Sing and Dance and Write It Away

Du Bois had now become the older guy hanging around all the young artists up in Harlem. On March 21, 1924, he'd gone to a club to see a bunch of young poets and novelists who were supporters of his. This event is where he'd meet many of the young Black artists who would form what's now known as the Harlem Renaissance, and Du Bois wanted to make sure they used their art to advance Black people by getting White people to respect them. It was a new form of uplift suasion—media suasion—which basically just means using media, in this case, art, to woo Whites.

But not everyone was kissing Du Bois's assimilationist feet. There was a resistant group of artists that emerged in 1926 who called themselves the Niggerati. They believed they should be able to make whatever they wanted to express themselves as whole humans without worrying about White acceptance. One of the Niggerati's most prominent poets was Langston Hughes, who declared that if a Black artist leaned toward Whiteness, his art wouldn't truly be his own. That it was okay to be a Black artist without having to feel insecurity or shame. They wanted to function the same way as the blues women, like Ma Rainey and Bessie Smith, who sang about pain and sex and whatever else they wanted to. Even if the images of Blackness weren't always positive. W. E. B. Du Bois and his supporters of uplift suasion and media suasion had a hard time accepting any narrative of Black people being less than perfect. Less than dignified. But the Niggerati were arguing that, if Black people couldn't be shown as imperfect, they couldn't be shown as human. And that was racist.

It would be up to Black artists to show themselves. To write and paint and dance and sculpt their humanity, whether White people liked it or not. Whether White people saw them as human or not. And they didn't see them as human. Instead, Black people were symbols, animals, and ideas to be feared. As a matter of fact, in 1929, three years after the formation of the Niggerati, Claude G. Bowers, an editor for the *New York Post*, confirmed this in a book he wrote called *The Tragic Era: The Revolution After Lincoln*.

Lincoln? Lincoln?! Abraham Lincoln had been dead for more than sixty years. But Reconstruction, if spun correctly, could be used as a way to play upon the hatred of racist White people. This was a way Bowers could tap back into the old days. Drum up that old hateful feeling. Rev the engine of racism, which, by the way, was still just as alive and consistent (which is why antiracist artists like the Niggerati found it silly to play into White comfort). Bowers was angry about the fact that Herbert Hoover, a Republican, swept the election in 1928 (remember the *switcheroo*), snatching several southern states. *The Tragic Era* was meant to remind Democrats, southerners, and racists that innocent White people were tortured by Black Republicans during Reconstruction. It's almost laughable. Almost. But it charged up racists and even sparked a re-release of the racist classic *Birth of a Nation*.

The argument of the savage, inferior Black person rides again. (It's getting exhausting, right?) And this time, Du Bois, who'd been slowly inching toward antiracism, decided to respond to the Bowers book. Du Bois wrote and published what he thought was his best work, *Black Reconstruction in America: 1860–1880*. In it he debunked all of Bowers's arguments and described how, if anything, Reconstruction was stifled by White racist elites who created more White privileges for poor White people as long as they stood, shoulder to shoulder, on the necks of Black people. Whiteness first. Always Whiteness first.

It was 1933. Du Bois's life as an assimilationist had finally started to vaporize. He just wanted Black people to be self-sufficient. To be Black. And for that to be enough. Here he argued that the American educational system was failing the country because it wouldn't tell the truth about race in America, because it was too concerned with protecting and defending the White race. Ultimately, he was arguing what he'd been arguing in various different ways, and what Frederick Douglass, Sojourner Truth, Booker T. Washington, Ida B. Wells-Barnett, Marcus Garvey, and many others before him had argued ad nauseam: that Black people were human.

Despite uplift suasion.

Despite media suasion.

Despite the fact that the NAACP was under new leadership, Walter White, who had decided to lean *more* into uplift suasion. White wanted to transform the NAACP into an organization of "refined" folks like himself, whose mission was to go before courts and politicians to persuade the White judges and legislators to end racial discrimination. But in 1933, Du Bois wanted nothing to do with this method.

He had finally turned away from assimilationism.

He had finally turned toward antiracism.

So, he took off from the NAACP, escaping the madness and bureaucracy, and headed down to Atlanta University to teach. He'd taken up a new school of thought. Inspired by Karl Marx, Du Bois broke ground on a new idea—antiracist socialism. He used this idea to move further into antiracism, even critiquing Black colleges for having White-centered curriculums or for having White teachers teaching Negro studies in Black schools.

The reason he'd turned such a sharp corner was, perhaps, because the country had entered into the Great Depression. No one had money. But it's one thing to have no money. It's another thing to have no money *and* no freedom. So Black people were experiencing a kind of double Depression. And even though the sitting president, Franklin D. Roosevelt, a Democrat, had developed an initiative called the New Deal, a flurry of government relief programs and job programs to keep people afloat, Black people needed their own New Deal to keep them safe from the old deal, which was the racist deal, which was no deal at all.

(Note: This was the start of the shift, where the Democratic and Republican parties start transforming into the ones we have today.)

It's not that the New Deal didn't help Black people at all. It did. Just not enough, and not at the same rate as it helped White people. And while poor Black people were trying to build their own systems, and as elite Black people were uncomfortable and pushing back against Du Bois, he published an article that would rock everyone.

It was 1934. The piece was called "Segregation." Du Bois sided with his former rival, Marcus Garvey, stating that there is a place, maybe even an importance, to a voluntary nondiscriminatory separation. Basically, Du Bois was arguing for Black safe spaces. Spaces that would resist and fight against the media storm of racist ideas that came year after year. From the stereotype that Black people were sexually immoral or hypersexual. Or that Black households were absent of fathers, and that this family dynamic made them inferior. Or that skin tone and hair texture were connected to beauty and intelligence. Du Bois, without the support of his partners at the NAACP, the assimilationists who were once in line with him, wanted to combat it all.

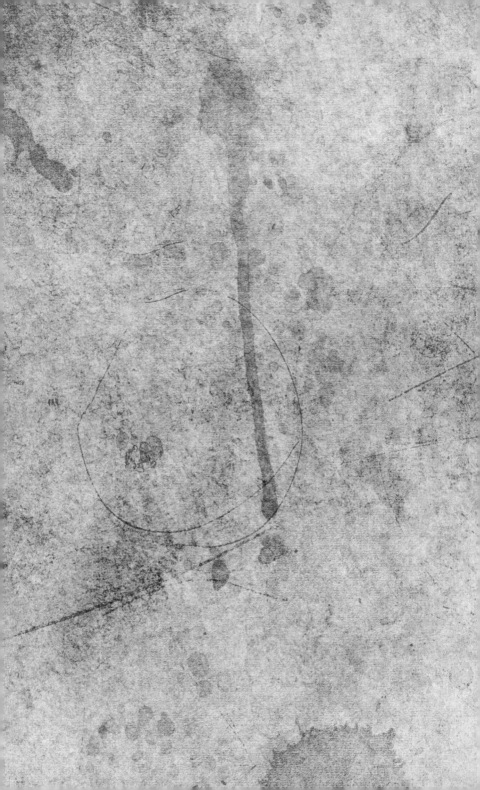

CHAPTER 20

Home Is Where the Hatred Is

WORLD WAR II.

I know, this isn't supposed to be a history book, but...come on.

After the United States entered World War II in 1942, Du Bois felt energized by Black America's "Double V Campaign": victory against racism at home and victory against fascism abroad. The Double V Campaign kicked the civil rights movement into high gear. And as World War II neared its end in April 1945, W. E. B. Du Bois joined representatives of fifty countries at the United Nations Conference on International Organization in San Francisco. He wanted the new United Nations Charter to become a buffer against racism. Then, later in the year, Du Bois attended the Fifth Pan-African Congress in Manchester, England. Pan-Africanism is a movement that encourages solidarity among all people of African descent. Strength in numbers. Global power. That was the key. At the Fifth Congress, in 1945, Du Bois was fittingly introduced as the "Father of Pan-Africanism."

In attendance were two hundred men and women, including Ghana's Kwame Nkrumah and Kenya's Jomo Kenyatta, young revolutionaries who would go on to lead the African decolonization movements, which were meant to remove colonial leaders. These delegates did not make the politically racist request of past pan-African congresses of gradual decolonization, as if Africans were not ready to rule Africans.

And what I mean when I mention "Africans ruling Africans" is Africans governing themselves. Imagine that. It must've felt like a bomb dropped on the heads of racist Europeans. Those weren't the only bombs dropping.

The United States emerged from World War II, looked over at the ravaged European and east Asian worlds, and flexed its unmatched capital, industrial force, and military arms as the new global leader. The only problem was, America, the land of the free, home of the brave, still had a race problem. And that race problem was starting to affect its relationships around the world. American freedom wasn't free. Hell, it wasn't even real. But no matter what compromises President Harry Truman (who took over after Roosevelt died in 1945) tried to make, the South always fought back.

I almost don't want to tell you what happened because I've told you what happened a lot already. But if you were to guess that White people started to perpetuate lies about Black people being inferior to keep the world of racism spinning, you'd be right.

On February 2, 1948, Truman urged Congress to implement a civil rights act, despite the lack of support among White Americans. You can imagine the outrage. Many left the Democratic Party. Others stayed and formed what they called the Dixiecrats, who, in order to fight back against Truman's push for civil rights, ran a man named Strom Thurmond for president. It was a grossly segregationist platform. Fortunately, it didn't work.

Black voters made sure Truman won, and once he did, his administration brought forth a few game-changing civil rights cases:

1. *Shelley v. Kraemer,* **1948**:

The case was decided with the Supreme Court determining that the courts could not enforce Whites-only real estate contracts in northern cities to keep out migrants and stop housing desegregation. This brought on the open housing movement, which basically exposed White people stopping Black people from living where they wanted to live. The fear was the same old fear. That Black people would make the neighborhoods dangerous. That their White daughters would be in danger. That the property value would go down. Some Black people wanted to live in White neighborhoods for validation. Some Black people were just looking for better housing options. Some White people were so afraid, they literally packed up and left their homes. White flight.

2. *Brown v. Board of Education,* **1954**:

I'm sure you've heard of this one. If you live in the South and go to a diverse school, this is why. This was the case that said racial segregation in public schools was unconstitutional. The results: The schools began to mix. What's really interesting about this case, though, something rarely discussed, is that it's actually a pretty racist idea. I mean, what it basically suggests is that Black kids need a fair shot, and a fair shot is in White schools. I mean, why weren't there any White kids integrating into Black schools? The assumption was that Black kids weren't as intelligent because they weren't around White kids, as if the mere presence of White kids would make Black kids better. Not. True. A good school is a good school, whether there are White people there or not. Oh, and of course people were pissed about this.

People were pissed about them both.

And pissed people do pissed things.

A year later, a fourteen-year-old boy named Emmett Till was brutally murdered in Money, Mississippi, for supposedly "hissing" at a White woman. They beat Till so ruthlessly that his face was unrecognizable during his open-casket funeral in his native Chicago. The gruesome pictures were shown around the enraged Black world, at the request of his mother. And though supremacists in power continued to blame *Brown v. Board of Education* for the problems, young Emmett's death lit a fire under the civil rights movement, led by a young, charismatic preacher from Atlanta who idolized W. E. B. Du Bois— Martin Luther King Jr.

There was a youthful energy to the movement. A new wave. A new way of doing things. And Du Bois loved watching it grow more and more powerful. He was now ninety years old, and hopeful. He'd never stopped struggling, and Dr. King was cut from similar cloth. He and Du Bois had not let up, and neither had college students. Four Black freshmen at North Carolina A&T entered a Woolworth's in Greensboro on February 1, 1960. They sat down at the "Whites only" counter, where they were denied service, and stayed there until the store closed. Within days, hundreds of students from area colleges and high schools were "sitting in." News reports of these nonviolent sit-ins flashed on TV screens nationally, setting off a sit-in wave to desegregate south- ern businesses. By April, students were staging sit-ins in seventy-eight southern and border communities, and the Student Non-Violent Coordinating Committee (SNCC) had been established. These college kids were like *new* New Negroes. They weren't waiting for White saviors, not in politicians like John F. Kennedy, who was running for office, or writers like Harper Lee, whose novel *To Kill a Mockingbird* was basically the *Uncle Tom's Cabin* of the civil rights movement. Don't mind if I . . . don't.

Nope, no White saviors for them. But they also weren't interested in being Black saviors. They weren't necessarily "saving" themselves. They were just "being" themselves. But the thing about being Black is that just being can bring bloodshed.

And that's what Dr. King, and the SNCC, and the civil rights movement as a whole were banking on.

The vicious violence in response to the nonviolent civil rights movement was embarrassing the country, all around the non-White world.

On April 3, 1963, King helped kick off a series of demonstrations in Birmingham, bringing on the wrath of the city's ruggedly segregationist police chief, "Bull" Connor. Nine days later, on Good Friday, eight White anti-segregationist Alabama clergymen signed a public statement requesting that these "unwise and untimely" street demonstrations end. Martin Luther King Jr., jailed that same day, read the statement from his cell. Angry, he started doing something he rarely did. He responded to critics, in his "Letter from Birmingham Jail," published that summer.

No one knows whether the sickly W. E. B. Du Bois read King's jailhouse letter. But just as Du Bois had done in 1903, and later regretted, in his letter King erroneously conflated two opposing groups: the antiracists who hated racial discrimination and the Black separatists who hated White people (in groups like the Nation of Islam). King later distanced himself from both, speaking to a growing split within the civil rights movement. More and more battle-worn young activists were becoming frustrated with King's nonviolence and were more often listening to Malcolm X's sermons. Malcolm X was a minister in the Nation of Islam, a religious organization focused on the liberation of Black people through discipline, self-defense, community organizing, and a fortified understanding of who Black people were regardless of White people's opinions. He preached that Blacks were the original people of the world, which pushed back against the Bible and the early theories of White

Egypt. He also preached Black self-sufficiency—that Black people could care for themselves, their families, and their communities all by themselves. Sure, he was a polarizing force, but he was also an antiracist persuading away assimilationist ideas.

On May 3, 1963, the young folks that followed leaders like Malcolm watched on television as Bull Connor's vicious bloodhounds ripped to pieces the children and teenagers of Black Birmingham, who had been following Dr. King; as Connor's fire hoses broke limbs, blew clothes off, and slammed bodies into storefronts; and as his officers clubbed marchers with nightsticks.

The world watched, too.

On June 11, President John F. Kennedy addressed the nation—or the world, rather—and summoned Congress to pass civil rights legislation. "Today we are committed to a worldwide struggle to promote and protect the rights of all who wish to be free," Kennedy said. "We preach freedom around the world, and we mean it."

With the eyes of the globe on him, Kennedy—who really didn't have much of a choice—introduced civil rights legislation. But it didn't stop the momentum of the long-awaited March on Washington for Jobs and Freedom. Though it had been organized by civil rights groups, the Kennedy administration controlled the event, ruling out civil disobedience. Kennedy aides approved the speakers and speeches—no Black women, no James Baldwin (an openly gay Black novelist who'd become a bold and brilliant political voice through his writings), and no Malcolm X. On August 28, approximately 250,000 activists and reporters from around the world marched to the area between the Lincoln Memorial and the Washington Monument. And King closed the day with what's probably the most iconic speech of all time—"I Have a Dream." But there was bad news. W. E. B. Du Bois had died in his sleep the previous day.

Indeed, a younger Du Bois had called for such a gathering, hoping it would persuade millions of White people to love the lowly souls of Black folk. And, yes, the older Du Bois had chosen another path—the antiracist path less traveled—toward forcing millions to accept the equal souls of Black folk. It was the path of civil disobedience that the young marchers in the SNCC and CORE (the Congress of Racial Equality, also responsible for much of the nonviolence training for the movement) had desired for the March on Washington, a path a young woman from Birmingham's Dynamite Hill was already traveling and would never leave. But Roy Wilkins, one of Dr. King's right-hand men, and the bearer of the bad news, did not dwell on the different paths. Looking out at the lively March on Washington, he just asked for a moment of silence to honor the ninety-five-year-old movement of a man.

SECTION

5

1963—TODAY

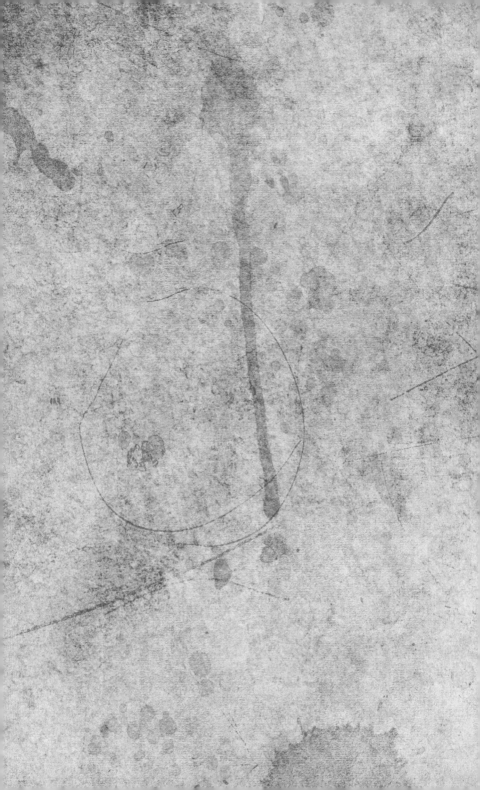

CHAPTER 21

When Death Comes

CYNTHIA WESLEY. CAROLE ROBERTSON. CAROL DENISE McNair. Addie Mae Collins.

These were the names of four girls killed in a church bombing.

It's September 16, 1963. The *Herald Tribune*. Angela Davis was a college student, a junior at Brandeis University, when she read these names in the newspaper—four girls killed in Birmingham, Alabama.

Angela Davis was from Birmingham. She knew these names. Her mother, Sallye, had taught Carol Denise in the first grade. The Robertson and Davis families had been close friends for as long as she could remember. The Wesleys lived around the block in the hilly Birmingham neighborhood where Angela grew up. Angela's mother wasn't deterred by the bombings. It was a frightening and painful moment, but the Davises were active, and by "active," I mean activists.

Sallye Davis had been a leader in the Southern Negro Youth Congress, an antiracist organization that protested racial and economic disparities. On Dynamite Hill, where Angela Davis grew up, Sallye and her husband trained their daughter to be an antiracist. And so most of her childhood was spent wrestling with the poverty and racism around her. Why didn't her classmates have certain things? Why were they hungry? Why weren't they able to eat in school? She even decided early on that she would never—despite the pressure—desire to be White.

She fought and spoke out all the way up until she got to college at Brandeis—a predominately White institution—where she didn't agree with the kind of activism going on. An activism laid out by White people who couldn't see that they weren't the standard. But she found her outlets. She found a place to put her activist energy.

James Baldwin, one of Davis's favorite authors, came to Brandeis in 1962, just before the release of his activist manifesto, *The Fire Next Time*. Baldwin crafted a collection of essays that encapsulated the Black experience with racism. The book contains a letter to his nephew, warning him of the oppression coming his way, and another letter addressing the centennial celebration of the Emancipation Proclamation, in which he charges both Black and White Americans to attack the nasty legacy of racism. It's a macro- and micro-examination of the American race machine, and ultimately a master class in antiracism.

Malcolm X also came, and though Davis didn't agree with his religious leanings, she really fell in line with his political ideas. She was fascinated by the way he explained the racism Black people had internalized, an inferiority complex forced on them by White supremacy.

But during Davis's junior year, while studying abroad in France, she was emotionally transported home when she read the four names in the *Tribune*. Cynthia Wesley. Carole Robertson. Carol Denise McNair. Addie Mae Collins. Back to Dynamite Hill.

Davis didn't see this moment as a special event, a one-off incident, no. She had grown up fully aware of American racism and its deadly potential. All she could do was swallow it and use it as fuel to keep fighting.

President John F. Kennedy, on the other hand, had to figure out how to fix it. Well, there was no fixing it, but at least he had to do something to snuff out what could become a complete explosion on Dynamite Hill.

He launched an investigation, which, by the way, caused his approval ratings to drop. Can you believe that? Four children were killed. Bombed. And because the president tried to get to the bottom of it, his southern constituents and supporters were actually upset. Kennedy tried to rebound. Tried to boost his ratings back up in Dallas two months later. He never made it back to the White House.

Two days after Kennedy's burial, Lyndon Baines Johnson, who was now president, proclaimed that the civil rights bill that Kennedy had been working on would be passed.

But what did that mean?

On paper it would mean that discrimination on the basis of race was illegal. But what it *actually* meant was that White people, even those in favor of it (in theory), could then argue that everything was now fine. That Black people should stop crying and fighting and "get over" everything, because now things were equal. It meant they'd argue what they'd been arguing, that Black people's circumstances are caused solely by themselves, and if they just worked harder and got educations, they'd succeed. It meant they'd completely ignore the hundreds of years of head starts White people had in America. And the worst part, the Civil Rights Act of 1964 would've caused White people to rethink White seniority and superiority, and instead of dealing with it, they'd turn it on its head, flip it around, do the old okey-doke and claim that they were now the victims. That they were being treated unfairly. Unjustly. So, even though the act was supposed to outlaw discrimination, it ended up causing a backlash of more racist ideas.

Nonetheless, the Civil Rights Act of 1964 was the first important civil rights legislation since the Civil Rights Act of 1875. Hours after President Johnson signed it into law, on July 2, 1964, he hit the TV screen to play up the whole American ideal of freedom. His appearance on television may as well have been a sitcom. A show, fully cast with the best actors, complete with smiling faces and a laugh track. And Black Americans, at least those who'd seen the show before, looked on, entertained, but fully aware it was all scripted.

And...*cut!*

Malcolm X, full of distrust for America, spoke out not against the bill but about the likelihood of its actually ever being enforced. Who was going to make sure the laws would be followed if the law, lawmakers, and law enforcers were all White and racist? Angela Davis felt the same way. And Angela and Malcolm weren't wrong. This was a political play. President Johnson knew that since he'd made it about Kennedy, this bill wouldn't hurt his position as president or his potential to get reelected. At least, that's what he thought. But George Wallace, the governor of Alabama and ultimate racist, threw a major wrench into Johnson's reelection plans. Wallace had taken a public stand *for* segregation the year before, and received 100,000 letters of support, mostly from northerners.

Wait. What? Yep. Northerners. Sending in letters in support of Wallace's stance *for* segregation. This proved, painfully, that everyone—the North and the South—hated Black people.

Barry Goldwater, a senator from Arizona, was also running. Goldwater was ushering in a new kind of conservatism. His platform was that government assistance, which White people had been receiving for a *long* time, was bad for human beings. That it turned people into animals. Of course, this racist epiphany hit Goldwater once Black people started receiving government assistance, too. Funny how that happens. Yet not funny at all. It's like someone telling you they hate your shoes, and then a week later, once they've put you down and made you feel insecure, they start wearing them. This strange game of whatever's good for the goose *not* being good for the gander. A gander is a male goose. But for this example, a gander is a whole bunch of Black people.

But Goldwater, despite the support he had from

well-to-do Whites, didn't worry Johnson, either. Johnson was concerned about the Black political movements, like the Mississippi Freedom Democratic Party and the Student Non-Violent Coordinating Committee, who weren't satisfied with what Johnson was doing for them. The northern activists had been dealing with and protesting police brutality and exploitation. The southern activists had survived, and were continuing to survive, the Klan. And what did Johnson offer them? What leverage did he grant the SNCC and MFDP? Two seats at the Democratic National Convention, which was basically nothing. No power. And without power, all the protesting in the world meant nothing. The shift went from fighting for civil rights to fighting for freedom. The difference between the two is simple. One implies a fight for fairness. The other, a right to live.

Malcolm X's empowerment philosophy of Black national and international unity, self-determination, self-defense, and cultural pride started to sound like music to the ears of the SNCC youth. At the end of 1964, Malcolm X returned from an extended trip to Africa to a growing band of SNCC admirers and a growing band of enemies. Unfortunately, a few months later—February 21, 1965—at a Harlem rally, Malcolm would be gunned down by those enemies.

When James Baldwin heard the news in London, he was devastated.

When Dr. Martin Luther King heard the news in Selma, Alabama, he was calm. Reflective. Acknowledged that, though they didn't always agree on methods— much like Du Bois and Washington, and Du Bois and Garvey—they wanted the same thing.

Malcolm X's death rocked the Black antiracist followers, especially the ones populating urban environments. He'd instilled a sense of pride, a sense of intellectual prowess, a sense of self into many. He'd made street guys feel that they had a place in the movement. He gave athletes like Muhammad Ali a higher purpose than boxing. He'd debated and deconstructed racism with a fearlessness many people had never seen, and his ideas evolved into a more inclusive Constitution just before the end of his life.

The media, however...well, the media did what the media had been doing for decades...centuries. They spun his entire life into a boogeyman tale, devoid of context. "Malcolm X's life was strangely and pitifully wasted," read a *New York Times* editorial.

But antiracists honored him and would have something to hold on to forever to reference his ideas. Alex Haley had been working with Malcolm on his autobiography, and the book would be published after his death. His ideological transformation, from assimilationist to anti-White separatist to antiracist, inspired millions. He argued that though White people weren't born racist, America was built to make them that way. And that if they wanted to fight against it, they had to address it with the other racist White people around them. He critiqued Black assimilationists. Called them puppets, especially the "leaders" who had exploited their own people to climb the White ladder. Malcolm X stamped that he was for truth—not hate—truth and truth alone, no matter where it was coming from. His autobiography would become antiracist scripture. It would become one of the most important books in American history.

President Johnson, still dealing with the hate (from White people) and the distrust (from Black people) around the Civil Rights Act, decides to go even further than that bill. Decides to double down. Dig his heels into the antiracist mud. After the Civil Rights Act came the Voting Rights Act of 1965. And though it would cause what every bit of progress caused, White rage and resistance, the Voting Rights Act would become the most effective piece of antiracist legislation ever passed by the Congress of the United States of America.

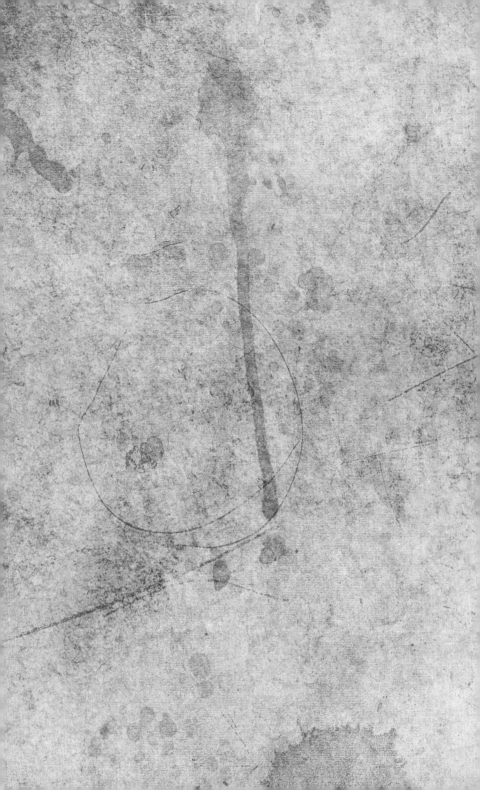

CHAPTER 22

Black Power

DIDN'T TAKE LONG FOR THE MUTATED RACISM TO SHOW up, but it also didn't take long for the mutated rebellion to meet that racism and look it square in the eye. Actually, it was met with a little more than a mean look. See, five days after the Voting Rights Act was signed into law, a social bomb exploded in the Watts neighborhood of Los Angeles when a police incident set off six days of violence. This became the deadliest and most destructive urban rebellion in history. Enough. Enough! There was no more picketing. No more marching. The squawking mockingbird had stopped its pecking and had transformed into a panther, brandishing teeth.

As Watts burned, Angela Davis boarded a boat headed for Germany to get her graduate degree in philosophy. Shortly after she arrived, in September 1965, an international group of scholars gathered in Copenhagen for the Race and Colour Conference. Davis didn't attend. But if she had, she would have heard lectures on the racist role of language symbolism. Scholars pointed out everyday phrases such as *black sheep*, *blackballing*, *blackmail*, and *blacklisting*, among others, that had long associated Blackness and negativity. Two other words could've been included—words that still exist today: *minority*, as if Black people are minor, making White people major; and *ghetto*, a term first used to describe an undesirable area of a city in which Jewish people were forced to live. But in the racist context of America, *ghetto* and *minority* became synonyms for *Black*. And all three of those words seemed to be knives.

That is, until people like Stokely Carmichael showed up.

Carmichael was born in Trinidad in 1941 and moved to the Bronx in 1952, the same year his idol, Malcolm X, was paroled from prison. In 1964, Carmichael graduated from Howard University. By then, Malcolm's disciples, including Carmichael, were saying that the word *Negro* was to describe Black assimilationists, and *Black* was for the antiracist, removing the ugliness and evil that had been attached to it. They were now passionately embracing the term *Black*, which stunned Martin Luther King Jr.'s "Negro" disciples and their own assimilationist parents and grandparents, who would rather be called "nigger" than "Black."

Carmichael was the kind of guy who'd rather be called dead than afraid. He was the new chairman of the SNCC. And a year after the uprising in Watts, he and the SNCC found themselves at a rally in Greenwood, Mississippi, called the March Against Fear. It was at this rally that Carmichael would exclaim a culture-shifting phrase. "What we gonna start saying now is Black Power!"

Black Power. And when Black people—especially the disenfranchised but also antiracist ones—caught wind of this phrase and married it to Malcolm X's autobiography (Black Power basically sums up the book), Black Power became a red fire burning in the Black community and burning down the White one. Well, maybe not burning it down, but definitely heating its butt.

What Stokely Carmichael meant by Black Power:

BLACK PEOPLE OWNING AND CONTROLLING THEIR OWN NEIGHBORHOODS AND FUTURES, FREE OF WHITE SUPREMACY.

What (racist) White people (and media) heard:

BLACK   SUPREMACY.

And once again, the mere notion of antiracist ideas got purposely jumbled into hateful extremism. There were even Black civil rights leaders, such as Roy Wilkins of the NAACP, who were against the Black Power mantra. Wilkins thought it was "reverse Mississippi," and "reverse Hitler." He would've been one of the Black people Malcolm X referred to as a Negro.

Despite all the assimilationist vomit coming from the Black elites and the racist vomit coming from White segregationists, Carmichael and his Black Power mantra pushed on. He traveled around the country, speaking, building the movement. But another movement was sprouting up at the same time.

Oakland, California. Two frustrated young men started their own two-man movement. They called themselves the Black Panther Party for Self Defense.

I'm sure you've seen the photos. These days they're on T-shirts and posters, randomly plastered around places as if the Black Panthers were Disney. They weren't. The black hats and leather jackets, the sunglasses and guns all were real. Huey P. Newton and Bobby Seale weren't characters. They were men, fed up. So they composed a ten-point platform of things they were fighting for in the newly founded Black Panther Party for Self Defense.

The Ten-Point Platform (paraphrased):

1. Power to determine the destiny of our Black community.

2. Full employment.

3. An end to the robbery of the Black community by the government.

4. Decent housing.

5. Real education.

6. For all Black men to be exempt from military service.

7. An immediate end to police brutality and murder of Black people.

8. Freedom for all Black prisoners.

9. For all Black people on trial to be tried by a jury of their peers.

10. Peace, and Black representation in the United Nations.

In the next few years, the Black Panther Party spread in chapters across the country, attracting thousands of committed and charismatic young community members. They policed the police, provided free breakfast for children, and organized medical services and political education programs, among a series of other initiatives.

And with the Black Panther Party growling, and the Black Power movement howling, Angela Davis was in Germany reading about it all. Finally, when she couldn't take being outside the action any longer, she packed up and moved back to America.

It was the summer of 1967, and Angela Davis was bound for California. The University of California, San Diego, to be exact. And as soon as she got there, she settled in and ramped up the Black Power movement, immediately starting a Black Student Union (BSU) on campus.

Wherever there were Black students, they were building BSUs or taking over student governments, requesting and demanding an antiracist and relevant education at historically Black *and* historically White colleges.

All sorts of different minds engaged with Black Power. Separatists, pan-Africanists, and everything in between. Black Power even appealed to the face of the civil rights movement. That's right, even Dr. King, in 1967, was turning away from assimilationist thought in the same way W. E. B. Du Bois had later in his life. Dr. King had now realized that desegregation was good only for elite Black people, while everyone else was harmed by it. It left millions drowning in poverty. So King switched gears and started planning the Southern Christian Leadership Conference's Poor People's Campaign. His goal was to bring poor people to Washington, DC, in order to force the government to pass an "economic bill of rights" committing to full employment, guaranteed income, and affordable housing, a bill that sounded a lot like the economic proposals in the Black Panther Party's ten-point platform.

Of course King was criticized. By his own people.

Of course White rage and fear sparked up. Too many protests. Civil rights. Poor people. Vietnam War. *Too. Many. Protests.*

Of course there was a moment in the media, a pop culture phenomenon like *The Birth of a Nation* or *Tarzan*, to send a message to White people to take up arms and be afraid, and also to send a shock through the confident backbone of Black America, to remind them of their place. This time, in 1968, the movie was called *Planet of the Apes*.

Here's the basic plot:

1. White astronauts land on a planet after a two-thousand-year journey.

2. Apes enslave them.

3. Turns out, they're not on a faraway planet at all. They're on Earth.

4. *(Noooooooooooooooooo!)*

While *Tarzan* put the racist conquering of Africa and Africans on the screen, *Planet of the Apes* stoked the racist fear fire by showing the dark world rising against the White conqueror. And just like with *Tarzan*, *Planet of the Apes* went boom. Became a megahit, complete with sequels and comics and merchandise. And just like that, the conversation coming from the American government shifted to protect *their* "planet." Black Power was met by a new slogan, one spat out like a racist slur. Law and order.

A week later, on April 4, Angela Davis was at the new office of the SNCC in Los Angeles. The newly organized SNCC chapter was her new activist home as she shuffled back and forth between Los Angeles and her doctoral studies at UC San Diego. That afternoon, she heard a scream. Following the scream came the news. Dr. King, after giving a speech that referenced a "human rights revolution," had been shot dead.

King's death transformed countless doubly conscious activists into singly conscious antiracists, and Black Power suddenly grew into the largest American antiracist movement ever. There was a shift happening.

James Brown made a song that insisted everyone "Say It Loud—I'm Black and I'm Proud." Black people started to move away from colorism, and some reversed. The darker, the better. The kinkier the hair, the better. The more African the clothing, the better.

From 1967 to 1970, Black students and their hundreds of thousands of non-Black allies compelled nearly a thousand colleges and universities spanning almost every

US state to introduce Black Studies departments, programs, and courses. The demand for Black Studies filtered down into K–12 schools, too, where textbooks still often presented African Americans as subhuman, happy slaves. Early Black Studies intellectuals went to work on new antiracist textbooks. Black Studies, and Black Power ideas in general, also began to inspire antiracist transformations among non-Blacks. White hippies, who had been anti–Vietnam War, had now begun pledging to (try to) strip the influence of racism from White Americans. Puerto Rican antiracists and the emerging Brown Power movement, which also challenged the color hierarchy. And while the movement continued to grow, Angela Davis was dipping her toe in different waters.

See, the Black Power movement wasn't perfect, of course. And though it had a righteous cause, it was still sexist. Men ran it all. Women were pushed to the back, like they'd been in every racial liberation movement in history. So, Davis started seriously considering joining the Communist Party, which at the time was feared by the American government, who thought the Communists (and communism, which was rooted in ending social classes) would overthrow democracy. Davis, a subscriber to the Communist ideals of revolution, felt the

Communist Party hadn't paid enough attention to race. But there was a collective of Communists of color that did. The Che-Lumumba Club. They were all it took to push her over the edge and join the Party. Her first role was working on the campaign for the first Black woman to run for the US presidency, the Communist Party candidate Charlene Mitchell.

In the 1968 presidential election, Mitchell squared off against Lyndon Johnson's vice president, Hubert Humphrey. Richard Nixon ran on the Republican ticket. His innovative campaign would reveal the future of racist ideas.

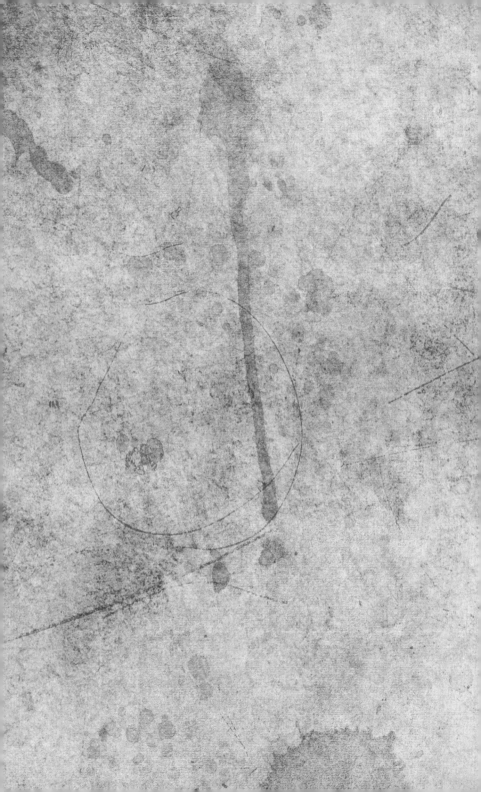

CHAPTER 23

Murder Was the Case

RICHARD NIXON AND HIS TEAM LOOKED AT THE WAY George Wallace had run his campaign (*Vote for Hate!*) and felt like it was a good idea to follow in his footsteps. Nixon believed the segregationist approach was a good one because it would lock down all the true-blue segregationists. Like, the varsity squad of racists. Along with those, Nixon figured he could also attract the White people who were afraid of…everything Black. Black neighborhoods. Black schools. Black…people. And the brilliant game plan (*ugh*) Nixon used to drive an even bigger wedge and get racists on his side was to simply demean Black people in every speech, while also praising White people. But the magic trick in it all—the "how did you hide that rabbit in that hat?" part—was that he did all this without ever actually saying "Black people" and "White people."

It goes back to things like the word *ghetto*.

And today, maybe you've heard *urban*.

Or how about *undesirables*?

Oh, and my favorite (not), *dangerous elements*.

Which would eventually become *thugs*.

My mother would call this "gettin' over," but for the sake of this *not history* history book, let's go with what the historians have named it: the "southern strategy." And, in fact, it was—and remained over the next five decades—the national strategy Republicans used to unite northern and southern racists, war hawks, and fiscal and social conservatives. The strategy was right on time. With the southern strategy in full tilt, and with the messaging being all about law and order—which meant doing anything to shut down protests, or at least to paint them as bloodbaths—Richard Nixon won the presidency.

In the fall of 1969, with Charlene Mitchell's campaign behind her, Angela Davis settled into a teaching position at the University of California, Los Angeles (UCLA). But the FBI had other plans. J. Edgar Hoover, the director of the FBI, had launched a war to destroy the Black

Power movement that year. And all they needed to cut Davis down was to know that she was part of the Communist Party. Ronald Reagan, the governor of California at the time, had her fired from UCLA. When she tried to plead her case, it set off a media storm. Hate mail started filling up her mailbox. She received threatening phone calls, and police officers started harassing her. And even though the California Superior Court would overturn her firing and allow her to go back to work, Reagan searched for new ways to get rid of her.

And he would succeed. The next time, he fired her for speaking out in defense of three Black inmates in Soledad State Prison who she felt were detained only because they were Black Power activists. Here's what happened. George Jackson was transferred to Soledad from San Quentin after disciplinary infractions. He had already served some years, after being accused of robbing a gas station of seventy dollars. His sentence for that crime— one year to life in prison. In 1970, a year after arriving in Soledad, Jackson and fellow Black inmates John Clutchette and Fleeta Drumgo were accused of murdering a prison guard in a racially charged prison fight. Whatever chance he had at freedom was now locked up with him behind bars.

Angela Davis had become friends with George Jackson's younger brother, Jonathan, who was committed to freeing his brother. They had been rallying. Angela Davis had been speaking. They had been fighting the good fight. But it wasn't enough for Jonathan Jackson, brother of George. He decided to take the freeing of his brother into his own hands.

This is real.

Pay attention.

It's gonna go quickly.

August 7, 1970.

Jonathan Jackson walked into a courtroom in California's Marin County.

He was holding three guns.

He took the judge, the prosecutor, and three jurors hostage.

He freed three inmates who were on trial.

He led the hostages to a van parked outside.

Police opened fire.

The shoot-out took the lives of the judge, two inmates, and also Jonathan Jackson.

He was seventeen years old.

A week later, Angela Davis was charged with murder.

Record scratch. Repeat.

A week later, Angela Davis was charged with murder. Because police said one of the guns Jonathan Jackson used was actually hers. If found guilty, she'd be sentenced to death. Angela went on the run. She was caught months later on the other side of the country. New York. October 13, 1970. She was arrested and brought to the New York Women's House of Detention. While she was in there, around so many other Black and Brown incarcerated women, she began to develop her Black feminist theory.

On the other side of the prison walls, organizations were fighting and rallying for her freedom. And this rallying cry continued after December 1970, when Davis was sent back to California, where she spent most of her jail time in solitary confinement, awaiting trial. She read the letters—thousands of letters—from activists and supporters. She also studied her case. Studied it and studied it and studied it. A year and a half later, her trial finally began.

She represented herself. And won.

On June 4, 1972, Angela Davis was free. But not. Not free in her own mind until she could help all the women and men she was leaving behind bars get free. There was no value, to her, in her own exceptionalism. She was an antiracist. She knew better than to beat her chest when there was a much bigger challenge to be beaten. Much stronger chains to break.

Three years later, Angela Davis returned to teaching. Nixon had resigned from office after a scandal he wasn't punished for (no surprise) and Gerald Ford was president. Just telling you that because you'd probably be wondering what happened to Nixon. Turns out, he was...a liar and couldn't, as my mother would say, *get over.* Anyway, Davis had taken a job at the Claremont Colleges Black Studies Center in Southern California, and she realized quickly that not much had changed since she'd been gone. Segregationists were still arguing some kind of natural-born problem with Black people.

And assimilationists were still trying to figure out why integration had failed. And the one thing that Black male assimilationist scholars kept arguing about was that Black masculinity was what was frightening to White men. That it was sexual jealousy that spawned systemic oppression, which is ridiculous, because it buys into the racist idea that Black men are sexually superior (making them superhuman, making them *not* human) and also continues the narrative that Black women just don't matter. Black women didn't have a place in the conversation, though they'd been the steadying stick from the moment the conversation began. All this is in line with decades—centuries!—of racist propaganda. Centuries of White men, and White women, and Black men, all working to erase or discredit who they thought posed the greatest threat to freedom, even if it's only—in the case of Black men—the freedom to pretend to be freer than they actually are.

And what about the LGBT community? Were they not to be included in this conversation? Fortunately there was...media. But not another *Tarzan* or *Planet of the Apes*. Not another *Uncle Tom's Cabin*, either. This time, just like with novelist Zora Neale Hurston, who had in the past written southern dialect into the mouths of strong women characters (*Their Eyes Were Watching God*), Black women were screaming with Black feminist, antiracist work.

Audre Lorde produced essays, stories, and poems from the perspective of being Black and lesbian. She pushed back against the idea that she, as a Black person, woman, and lesbian, was expected to educate White people, men, and/or heterosexuals in order for them to recognize her humanity.

Ntozake Shange used her creative, antiracist energy to produce a play, *For Colored Girls Who Have Considered Suicide/When the Rainbow Is Enuf*, portraying the lives of Black women and their experiences of abuse, joy, heartbreak, strength, weakness, love, and longing for love. Some people were afraid it would strengthen stereotypes of Black women. Some were afraid it would strengthen stereotypes of Black men. Both fears are code for the fear of an antiracist truth.

Alice Walker wrote *The Color Purple*, a novel that presents a Black woman dealing with abusive Black men, abusive southern poverty, and abusive racist Whites. The tired argument about the Black male stereotype arose again. But...so what?

And Michele Wallace wrote a book called *Black*

Macho and the Myth of the Superwoman. Wallace believed sexism was an even greater concern than racism. She was loved, but she was hated just as much.

And while the idea of Black masculinity was being challenged by Black women, White masculinity was being threatened, constantly, by Black men. So, once again, White America created a symbol of hope. Of "man." I mean, MAN. Of macho. Of victor. And plastered it on the big screen. Again. This time his name was Rocky.

I'm sure you've seen at least one of the movies, even if it's one of the new ones. And if you haven't, you know the fight song. The song playing while Rocky runs up a set of museum steps, training, tired, but triumphant. Yeah.

Rocky, played by Sylvester Stallone, was a poor, kind, slow-talking, slow-punching, humble, hardworking, steel-jawed Italian American boxer in Philadelphia, facing off against the unkind, fast-talking, fast-punching, cocky African American world heavyweight champion. I mean, really? Rocky's opponent, Apollo Creed (the new movies are about his son), with his amazing thunderstorm of punches, symbolized the empowerment movements, the rising Black middle class, and the real-life heavyweight champion of the world in 1976, the pride of Black Power masculinity, Muhammad Ali. Rocky symbolized the pride of White supremacist masculinity's refusal to be knocked out from the thunderstorm of civil rights and Black Power protests and policies.

Weeks before Americans ran out to see *Rocky*, though, they ran out to buy Alex Haley's *Roots: The Saga of an American Family*. Haley, who was known for working with Malcolm X on his autobiography, had now basically written the slave story of all slave stories. It was a seven-hundred-page book, then made into a miniseries that became the most watched show in television history. It blew up a bunch of racist ideas about how slaves were lazy brutes, mammies, and sambos, and how slave owners were benevolent and kind...landlords. But as much as antiracist Black Americans loved their *Roots*, racist White Americans loved—on and off screen—their Rocky, with his unrelenting fight for the law and order of racism. And then, in 1976, their Rocky ran for president.

CHAPTER 24

What War on Drugs?

NOT LIKE ROCKY, ROCKY. LIKE, NOT THE CHARACTER or the guy who played the character, Sylvester Stallone (though that would've been funny—or not). But it was, in fact, an actor. One who had already done damage to Black people. The one who'd been gunning for Angela Davis. Who kept her from working. That's right, Ronald Reagan was running for president. He'd lose the nomination to Gerald Ford in 1976 but would come right back in 1980 with a vengeance. He'd use an updated version of *law and order* politics and the southern strategy to address his constituents and talk about his enemies without ever having to say White or Black. He dominated the media (Angela Davis was running against him, for the vice president seat, and couldn't get any coverage), created false narratives about the state of the country, and won.

And lots of things unfolded. New, shaky propaganda that many people took seriously, about genetics coding us to be who we are. As if there were a gene for racism. New antiracist feminist thought coming from writers like bell hooks and, of course, Angela Davis. But nothing could prepare anyone for what was coming.

Two years into Reagan's presidency, he issued one of the most devastating executive orders of the twentieth century. The War on Drugs. Its role, maximum punishment for drugs like marijuana. This war was really one on Black people. At the time, drug crime was declining. As a matter of fact, only 2 percent of Americans viewed drugs as America's most pressing problem. Few believed that marijuana was even that dangerous, especially compared with the much more addictive heroin. But President Reagan wants to go to war? Against drugs?

If you're like me, you're asking yourself, *Was he on drugs?* Yes. Yes, he was. The most addictive drug known to America. Racism. It causes wealth, an inflated sense of self, and hallucinations. In this case, it would unfairly incarcerate millions of Black Americans. And in 1986, during his second term, Reagan doubled down on the

War on Drugs by passing the Anti–Drug Abuse Act. This bill gave a minimum five-year sentence for a drug dealer or drug user caught with five grams of crack, the amount typically handled by Blacks and poor people, while the mostly White and rich users and dealers of powder cocaine—who operated in neighborhoods with fewer police—had to be caught with five hundred grams to receive the same five-year minimum sentence.

Let that sink in.

Same drug. Different form.

One gets five years in prison if caught with five grams (the size of two quarters).

The other gets five years in prison for five hundred grams (the size of a brick).

The results should be obvious. Mass incarceration of Black people, even though White people and Black people were selling and using drugs at similar rates. Not to mention police officers policed Black neighborhoods more, and the more police, the more arrests. It's not rocket science. It's racism. And it would, once again, tear the Black community apart. More Black men were going to prison, and when (if) they came home, it was without the right to vote. No political voice. Also, no jobs. Not just because of felony charges, but because Reagan's economic policies caused unemployment to skyrocket. So violent crimes rose because people were hungry. And, according to Reagan and racists, it was all Black people's fault. Not the racist policies that jammed Black people up.

And the media, as always, drove the stereotypes without discussing the racist framework that created much of them. Once again, Black people were lazy and violent, the men were absent from the home because they were irresponsible and careless, and the Black family was withering due to all this, but especially, according to Reagan, because of welfare. There was no evidence to support any of this, but hey, who needs evidence when you have power, right?

The worst part is that everyone believed it. Even Black people. And to offset that image, or at least attempt to, another television show was created portraying the perfect Black family.

The Cosby Show.

A doctor and a lawyer with five children, in the upscale section of Brooklyn Heights. Upper middle class. Healthy marriage. Good parents. The father, Heathcliff Huxtable, played by Bill Cosby, even has his office in his home so that he never has to risk not being there for his children. There's the older, responsible daughter; the rebellious second daughter; the goofy but endearing son; the awkward and nerdy third daughter; and the cute, lovable baby girl. And their collective role as a family of extraordinary Negroes was to convince White people that Black families were more than what they were being portrayed to be. Which of course was racist in and of itself, because it basically said that if a Black family didn't operate like the Huxtables, they weren't worthy of respect.

And, of course, the Cosbys did nothing to slow Reagan's war. If anything, the show helped create a more polarizing view, because in 1989, a Pulitzer Prize–winning, Harvard medical degree–holding *Washington Post* columnist named Charles Krauthammer invented the term *crack baby*. It was a term used to blanket a generation of Black children born from drug-addicted parents, saying they were now destined for inferiority. That they were subhuman. That the drugs had changed their genetics. There was no science to prove any of this. But who needs science when you have racism? And that term, that label, *crack baby*, grew long arms and wrapped them around Black children all over the inner cities of America, whether it was true or not. Krauthammer and racists had basically figured out how to create a generation of criminals in their minds.

But Black people, as always, fought back. And this time, in the late eighties, after the election of George H. W. Bush (who of course used Reagan's racist ideas to win), they would beat racism back with...a beat.

CHAPTER 25

The Soundtrack
of Sorrow and
Subversion

1988.

My mic sounds nice. (Check one.)

My mic sounds nice. (Check two.)

Hip-hop had arrived. It had been about a decade since it was born in the South Bronx. BET and MTV started airing hip-hop shows. The *Source* magazine hit newsstands that year, beginning its reign as the world's longest-running rap periodical. But it was the music itself that was driving change and empowerment.

Here are a few songs from that year (check them out!):

Slick Rick: "Children's Story"

Ice-T: "Colors"

N.W.A.: "Straight Outta Compton"

Boogie Down Productions: "Stop the Violence"

Queen Latifah: "Wrath of My Madness"

Public Enemy: "Don't Believe the Hype"

It would be Public Enemy that really set the tone the following year. In 1989, they wrote a song that was placed in Spike Lee's Black rebellion movie *Do the Right Thing*. The song was a forceful mantra. An updated version of Stokely Carmichael's "Black Power!" and James Brown's "Say It Loud—I'm Black and I'm Proud." For the new generation of hip-hop heads and rebellious Black teenagers angry about racist mistreatment, it was Public Enemy's "Fight the Power."

And with all the Black feminist thought, including the work of Kimberlé Williams Crenshaw, who focused on the intersection between race and sex, women rappers like MC Lyte and Salt-N-Pepa took their place on the hip-hop stage. Actually, they fared better than women in Hollywood because at least their art was in mass circulation. Aside from Julie Dash's pioneering *Daughters of the Dust*, Black men were the only ones producing major Black films in 1991. These included illustrious films like Mario Van Peebles's *New Jack City*; John Singleton's debut antiracist tragedy, *Boyz N the Hood*; and Spike Lee's acclaimed interracial relationship satire, *Jungle Fever*.

Black men produced more films in 1991 than during all of the 1980s. But a White man, George Holliday, shot the most influential racial film of the year on March 3 from the balcony of his Los Angeles apartment. He was filming a twenty-five-year-old Black man, Rodney King, being brutally beaten by four Los Angeles police officers.

The public—the Black public—broke open. The levees holding back the waters of righteous indignation crumbled under the sight of those officers' batons.

How much more can we take?

How much more?

President Bush danced around the issue. Appointed a Black Supreme Court justice, Clarence Thomas, to replace Thurgood Marshall, as if that were supposed to pacify an angry and hurt Black community. And to make matters worse, Clarence Thomas was an assimilationist in the worst way. He saw himself as the king of self-reliance. A "pick yourselves up by the bootstraps" kind of guy, even though his work as an activist got him into his fancy schools and landed him this fancy job. And to add the racist cherry on top, Clarence Thomas had been accused by a woman named Anita Hill of sexual harassment when she served as his assistant at an earlier job. Nothing was done. No one believed her. In fact, she was persecuted.

So, in 1991, Angela Davis was reeling. Her year had started with the brutal beating of Rodney King (the cops were on trial at this point) and ended with the verbal lashing of Anita Hill (Thomas was confirmed as a Supreme Court justice anyway). As if the reminder that being Black and being a woman weren't enough of a double whammy, the year also ended for Davis in an unfamiliar place. She had taken a new professorship at the University of California, Santa Cruz, and stepped away from the Communist Party after spending twenty-three years as the most recognizable Communist in America. The Party refused to acknowledge the issues that Davis had fought so hard to bring to light. Racism. Sexism. Elitism. All things the Communist Party ultimately took part in perpetuating. So she left. But she didn't jump from Communist to Democrat. Or rather, a

New Democrat, as the party was going through a bit of an overhaul. A remix. A revamp. Fiscally liberal, but tough on welfare and crime. And the man leading this new Democratic Party was a dazzling, well-spoken, and calculating Arkansas governor named Bill Clinton.

It was 1992. And by the time the cops who had beaten Rodney King were found not guilty, Clinton had already run away with the Democratic nomination. But who could think about that when America had just told millions of people who had watched the Rodney King beating that those officers had done nothing wrong? So, Black people hit the L.A. streets in rebellion. It would take twenty thousand troops to stop them. Bill Clinton blamed both political parties for failing Black America while also blaming Black America and calling the people in the midst of the uprising—people in immense pain—lawless vandals.

About a month later, Clinton took his campaign to the national conference of Jesse Jackson's Rainbow Coalition. Though Jackson was widely unpopular among the racist Whites whom Clinton was trying to attract to the New Democrats, when Jackson invited the hip-hop artist Sister Souljah to address the conference, the Clinton team saw its political opportunity. The twenty-eight-year-old Bronx native had just released *360 Degrees of Power*, an antiracist album so provocative that it made Spike Lee's films and Ice Cube's albums seem like *The Cosby Show.*

And Clinton's response to Sister Souljah was that *she* was being racist. It was a political stunt, but it thrilled racist voters, and catapulted Clinton to a lead he'd never lose.

By the end of 1993, rappers were under attack. They were being criticized from all sides, not just from Bill Clinton. Sixty-six-year-old civil rights veteran C. Delores Tucker and her National Political Congress of Black Women took the media portrayals debate to a new racist level in their strong campaign to ban "gangsta rap." To her, rap music was setting Black people back. She felt like it was making Black people more violent, more materialistic, more sexual. To Tucker, the music was making its urban Black listeners inferior, though she never said anything about its suburban White listeners.

While Tucker focused on shutting down gangsta rap, the Massachusetts Institute of Technology historian Evelyn Hammonds mobilized to defend against the defamation of Black womanhood. More than two thousand Black female scholars from all across the country made their way to MIT's campus on January 13, 1994, for "Black Women in the Academy: Defending Our Name, 1894–1994." Among them was Angela Davis. She was the conference's closing speaker. She was certainly the nation's most famous Black American woman academic. But, more important, over the course of her career, she had consistently defended Black women, including those Black women who even some Black women did not want to defend. She had been arguably America's most antiracist voice over the past two decades, unwavering in her search for antiracist explanations when others took the easier and racist way of Black blame.

In her speech, she proposed a "new abolitionism," pushing for a rethinking of prisons and how they function. Ten days later, President Bill Clinton endorsed, basically, a new slavery. A "three strikes and you're out" law. It was called the Violent Crime Control and Law Enforcement Act, giving hard time to certain three-time offenders, which ended up causing the largest increase of the prison population in US history, mostly on nonviolent drug offenses. Mostly Black men. Of course, this once more put fuel in the "Black people are naturally criminals" vehicle, a vehicle that had been driving fast for a long time, running over everything in its path. But there was (another) academic debate brewing on whether Black people were natural or nurtured fools. And this particular debate had serious political repercussions for Clinton's tough-on-Blacks New Democrats, and the newest force in American politics, which pledged to be even tougher.

CHAPTER 26

A Million Strong

INTELLIGENCE. WHAT IS IT? THIS ISN'T A TRICK QUES-
tion. Or maybe it is. Either way, it was what academics
were talking about as Bill Clinton's crime laws drove the
unintelligent-Black narrative. What scholars were arguing is that intelligence is so relative, it's impossible to
actually measure fairly and without bias. Uh-oh. This
notion virtually shook the foundations of the racist ideas
that Black people were less intelligent than White people. Or that women were less intelligent than men. Or
that poor people were less intelligent than rich. It shook
the idea that White schools were better, and even poked
at the reason White students were perhaps going to
wealthy White universities—not because of intelligence

but because of racism. In the form of flawed and biased standardized testing.

Enter Richard Herrnstein and Charles Murray. Harvard guys. They wouldn't stand for this kind of talk. No, no, no. So they wrote a book refuting it all. It was called *The Bell Curve: Intelligence and Class Structure in American Life*. The book argued that standardized testing was real and valid and, most important, fair. Which then meant that Black people, who were disproportionately doing poorly on these tests, were intellectually inferior due to genetics or environment. (I wish there was something new to add. But, as you can see, the entire history was a recycling of the same racist ideas. Not the most original people, those racists.)

The year is 1994. And Herrnstein and Murray's book was published during the final stretch of the midterm elections. New Republicans issued their extremely tough "Contract with America" to take the welfare and crime issue back from Clinton's New Democrats. (Funny how all the new things feel so...old.) Charles Murray jumped on board and started to rally voters and campaign for the Republicans by encouraging and rationalizing the anti-welfare bill, called the Personal Responsibility and Work Opportunity Reconciliation Act.

Personal responsibility...hmmm.

This was another one of those *get-overs.*

The mandate was simple enough: Black people, especially poor Black people, needed to take "personal responsibility" for their economic situation and for racial disparities and stop blaming racism for their problems and depending on the government to fix them. It convinced a new generation of Americans that irresponsible Black people, not racism, caused the racial inequities. It sold the lie that racism has had no effect. So Black people should stop crying about it.

It became a game of one-ups. The Democrats were tough on crime and welfare. The Republicans got tougher. Then the Democrats got tougher. Then the Republicans got tougher. So tough that they tried, once more, to get Angela Davis fired after University of California, Santa Cruz's faculty awarded her the prestigious President's Chair professorship in January 1995. She was still a threat. But how could she be a threat while at the same time Republicans were claiming racism was over? What would she be threatening? What would she still be fighting? Why would she need to be fired?

Not to mention, 1995 was a year that made clear that racism was far from over.

I mean, 1995 was when the O. J. Simpson thing happened. The trial. I know you know about it. If not, he was accused of killing his wife and her friend, both White. The trial split the country in half, with Black people rooting for O. J.'s acquittal and White people rooting for his imprisonment. It was like watching the worst reality show of all time.

The year 1995 was when the term *super predator* was created by Princeton University scholar John J. Dilulio to describe Black fourteen- to seventeen-year-olds. Murder rates were up among that age range, but so was unemployment. Of course, Dilulio left that part out.

The year 1995 was also when the biggest political mobilization in Black American history took place. The Million Man March. It had been proposed by Louis Farrakhan, leader of the Nation of Islam. Though the march was powerful in its groundswell, it was flawed in its sexism, which Angela Davis spoke out against the day before the march.

The year 1995 was when activists would come together to defend the world's most famous Black male political prisoner, Mumia Abu-Jamal. He had been convicted of killing a White police officer in Philadelphia in

1982, though he claims innocence. A book of his commentaries was published that year, *Live from Death Row*. His execution was to be August 17, 1995, but because of the protests, Mumia was granted an indefinite stay of execution.

And where was Bill Clinton when all this was going on? Not at the Million Man March, that's for sure. He was in Texas, pleading to evangelicals for racial healing. Instead of listening to the people dealing with it, he went to beg people not dealing with it to ask God to fix it. And, of course, it slipped into *pray God fixes Black people*. Even though a year later, affirmative action was banned in California, making the playing field, especially as it pertained to higher education, more lopsided. The percentage of African Americans at University of California campuses began to decline, and the push for the end of affirmative action would spread, all under Bill Clinton's watch.

A year later, in June 1997, Clinton gave a commencement address at Angela Davis's alma mater, UC San Diego. It was as if suddenly he'd seen the light (the irony!) and pledged to lead "the American people in a great and unprecedented conversation on race."

Racial reformers applauded him.

And Black women had something to say. A nudge. You know, to get the conversation started.

And when I say Black women, what I mean is...one million of them.

On October 25, 1997, in Philadelphia, a million Black women gathered to have their voices heard. Congresswoman Maxine Waters, Sister Souljah, Winnie Mandela, Attallah and Ilyasah Shabazz (daughters of Malcolm X), and Dorothy Height all spoke. But so did White men. Not at the march, but in the media. And what they argued in response to Clinton's statements was that the way to fix racism was to stop focusing on it.

Wrong!

But that's what they said. And that sentiment set the tone for what would become "color blindness."

P A U S E.

Take a breath. How many of you know the "I have a Black friend" person, who then follows that statement with this one: "But I don't see color."

Yeah. U N P A U S E.

This color-blind rhetoric seemed to have its intended effect. Segregationists and assimilationists started favoring the color-blind product nearly a century after the

Supreme Court had ruled in favor of "separate but equal." And it had the same effect. Lip service. The millennium was coming, and people still couldn't fathom equality, because of color. But they used a new "multicultural" paint to brush over a racist stain. And a single coat wouldn't do.

CHAPTER 27

A Bill Too Many

WANT TO KNOW SOMETHING INCREDIBLE? AND STRANGE? And both surprising yet not surprising at all?

Scientific evidence that the races are 99.9 percent the same was brought forth on June 26, 2000. The year 2000 was when people were given scientific evidence that human beings were the same, despite the color of their skin. Isn't that wild?

Bill Clinton delivered the news as if it were news.

But Craig Venter, one of the scientists responsible, was more frank than Clinton in how he spoke about it. "The concept of race has no genetic or scientific basis," Venter said. His research team at Celera Genomics had determined "the genetic code" of five individuals, who were identified as either "Hispanic, Asian, Caucasian, or African American," and the scientists could not tell one race from another.

But there was 0.1 percent still out there. And that 0.1 percent difference between humans *must* be racial. Whether it is or isn't, it was going to be exploited by racist scientists who did everything they could to provide evidence that the races were biologically different. First curse theory and polygenesis, and now genes—racists were relentless.

But they didn't get much traction. Months later, the United States Report to the United Nations Committee on the Elimination of Racial Discrimination pointed out what was now the broken US race record: There had been "substantial successes," but there were "significant obstacles" remaining. It was September 2000, and Texas governor George W. Bush was pledging to restore "honor and dignity" to the White House, while Vice President Al Gore was trying to distance himself from Bill Clinton's impeachment scandal. The report's findings of discrimination and disparities across the American board did not become campaign talking points, as they reflected poorly on both the Clinton administration and the Republicans' color-blind America. Science says the races are biologically equal. So, if they're not equal in society, the only reason why can be racism.

And it played out again in the law a few months later, when tens of thousands of Black voters in Governor Jeb Bush's Florida were barred from voting or had their votes destroyed, allowing George W. Bush to win his brother's state by fewer than five hundred votes. This racist act would end up leading George W. Bush to the presidency.

But once in office, he also couldn't stop the antiracist momentum. The reparations conversation had kicked into high gear, and nearly twelve thousand women and men ventured to beautiful Durban, South Africa, for the United Nations World Conference Against Racism, Racial Discrimination, Xenophobia and Related Intolerance, held from August 31 to September 7, 2001. Delegates passed around a report on the prison-industrial complex and women of color that had been coauthored by Angela Davis. They also identified the Internet as the latest mechanism for spreading racist ideas, citing the roughly sixty thousand White supremacist sites and the racist statements so often made in comments sections following online stories about Black people. The United States had the largest delegation, and antiracist

Americans established fruitful connections with activists from around the world, many of whom wanted to ensure that the conference kicked off a global antiracist movement. As participants started venturing back to Senegal, the United States, Japan, Brazil, and France around September 7, 2001, they carried their antiracist momentum around the world.

And then it all came crashing down. Literally. September 11, 2001. After about three thousand Americans heartbreakingly lost their lives in attacks on the World Trade Center, on the Pentagon, on United Airlines Flight 93 that went down in Pennsylvania, President Bush condemned the "evil-doers," the insane "terrorists," all the while promoting anti-Islamic and anti-Arab sentiments. Color-blind racists exploited the raw feelings in the post-9/11 moment, playing up a united, patriotic America, where anyone who wasn't waving a flag was in fact an enemy to the country.

But there was no united front. Not in the broad scheme of things. Affirmative action was still being challenged, and no one wanted to grapple with the fact that the issue with education could be better dealt with if the racial preferences of standardized testing were eradicated. But the use of standardized testing *grew* in

K–12 schooling when the Bush administration's bipartisan No Child Left Behind Act took effect in 2003. The premise was simple. Set high goals and test often to see if those goals are being met. And then fund the schools based on those results. And though it was called No Child Left Behind, it actually encouraged mechanisms that *decreased* funding to schools when students were not making improvements, thus leaving the neediest students behind. It once again put the blame on Black children. And Black teachers. And public schools. Not on racist policies.

And the worst part is that Black assimilationists bought in once more. People like Bill Cosby, who blamed Black parents. "The lower economic people are not holding up their end in this deal. These people are not parenting," Cosby said in Washington, DC, after being honored at an NAACP gala in May 2004. "They are buying things for kids. Five-hundred-dollar sneakers for what? And they won't spend two hundred dollars for Hooked on Phonics. I am talking about these people who cry when their son is standing there in an orange suit."

And while Bill Cosby took his racist ideas on the road for a speaking tour, a rising star of the Democratic

Party, Barack Obama, subverted Cosby's message during his keynote address at the Democratic National Convention in Boston on July 27, 2004. "Go into any inner-city neighborhood, and folks will tell you that government alone can't teach kids to learn. They know that parents have to teach, that children can't achieve unless we raise their expectations and turn off the television sets and eradicate the slander that says a black youth with a book is acting white. They know those things." A booming applause interrupted Obama as his takedown of Cosby's critique settled in. Obama presented himself as a racial and socioeconomic unicorn. Humble beginnings and a lofty ascent. Both native and immigrant ancestry. Also, both African and European ancestry. He checked every box. And though at the time he was campaigning for John Kerry (who would lose the election to George W. Bush), it was clear a star was born.

CHAPTER 28

A Miracle and
Still a Maybe

Two weeks after his exhilarating keynote address, Barack Obama's memoir, *Dreams from My Father: A Story of Race and Inheritance*, was republished. It rushed up the charts and snatched rave reviews in the final months of 2004. Toni Morrison, the queen of American letters and the editor of Angela Davis's iconic memoir three decades earlier, deemed *Dreams from My Father* "quite extraordinary." Obama had written the memoir in the racially packed year of 1995 as he prepared to begin his political career in the Illinois Senate.

In the book, he claimed to be exempt from being an "extraordinary Negro," but racist Americans of all colors would in 2004 begin hailing Barack Obama, with all his public intelligence, morality, speaking ability, and political success, as such. The "extraordinary Negro" hallmark had come a mighty long way from Phillis Wheatley to Barack Obama, who became the nation's only African American in the US Senate in 2005. With Phillis Wheatley, racists despised the capable Black mind, but with Obama, they were turning their backs on history so that they could see him as a symbol of a post-racial America. An excuse to say the ugliness is over.

But it was a devastating natural and racial disaster that summer that would burst the bubble of post-racial make-believe, and if anything, forced a tense debate about racism. During the final days of August 2005, Hurricane Katrina took more than 1,800 lives, forced millions to migrate, flooded the beautiful Gulf Coast, and caused billions in property damage. Hurricane Katrina blew the color-blind roof off America and allowed all to see—if they dared to look—the dreadful progression of racism.

For years, scientists and journalists had warned that if southern Louisiana took "a direct hit from a major hurricane," the levees could fail and the region—a poor

Black community—would be flooded and destroyed. No one did anything.

And once it happened, the response from the Federal Emergency Management Agency (FEMA) was delayed. It was rumored that the Bush administration directed FEMA to delay its response in order to amplify the destructive reward for those who would benefit. Whether or not this is true, they were delayed. And people were drowning. It took three days to deploy rescue troops to the Gulf Coast region, more time than it took to get troops on the ground to quell the 1992 Rodney King rebellion. And then came the media. This time spinning tales of looting and gruesome, sensationalized stories of children in the Superdome (where people were being sheltered) having their throats cut.

In the era of color-blind racism, no matter how gruesome the racial crime, no matter how much evidence was stacked against them, racists were standing before the judge and pleading "not guilty." But how many criminals actually confess when they don't have to? From "civilizers" to standardized testers, assimilationists have rarely confessed to racism. Enslavers and Jim Crow segregationists went to their graves claiming innocence. And just as many presidents before him have, including Reagan, Lincoln, and Jefferson, George W. Bush will likely do the same.

On February 10, 2007, Barack Obama stood in front of the Old State Capitol building in Springfield, Illinois, and formally announced his presidential candidacy. He stood on the same spot where Abraham Lincoln had delivered his historic "House Divided" speech in 1858. Obama brimmed with words of American unity, hope, and change. No one saw him coming. As a matter of fact, everyone said Hillary Clinton was the inevitable choice, until Obama came through Iowa and snatched it from under her nose. By February 5, 2008, Super Tuesday (the Tuesday in the presidential election season when the greatest number of states hold primary elections), Americans had been swept up in the Obama "Yes We Can" crusade of hope and change, themes he embodied and spoke about so eloquently in his speeches that people started to hunger for him. But in mid-February, his perceptive and brilliant wife, Michelle Obama, told a Milwaukee rally, "For the first time in my adult life, I am really proud of my country, and not just because Barack has done well, but because I think people are hungry for change." That's all racists needed to pounce and call her unpatriotic. To try to tear the Obamas down and discredit them. Racist commentators became obsessed with Michelle Obama's body, her near-six-foot, chiseled, and curvy frame simultaneously semi-masculine and hyperfeminine. They searched for problems in her Black marriage and family, calling them extraordinary when they did not find any.

Then they found a scapegoat in one of Black America's most revered liberation theologians, the recently retired pastor of Chicago's large Trinity United Church of Christ—Jeremiah Wright. He'd officiated at the Obamas' wedding and spoke honestly about his feelings for a country that had worked overtime to kill him and his people. But the media used Wright's critiques of America to slander Obama.

Obama tried to brush it off. Tried to downplay his relationship with Pastor Wright, but nothing was working. So, instead, he delivered the speech of his life. It was called "A More Perfect Union." It was a speech on race, and it teetered back and forth between painful assimilationist thought and bold antiracism.

And it worked. It pushed him on, past the barrage of obstacles to come, including the one fueled by Donald

Trump that challenged whether or not Obama was an American.

And on November 4, 2008, a sixty-four-year-old recently retired professor, Angela Davis, cast a vote for a major political party for the first time in her voting life. She had retired from academia but not from her very public activism of four decades. She was still traveling the country trying to rouse an abolitionist movement against prisons. In casting her vote for Democrat Barack Obama, Davis joined roughly 69.5 million Americans. But more than voting for the man, Davis voted for the grassroots efforts of the campaign organizers, those millions of people demanding change.

When the networks started announcing that Obama had been elected the forty-fourth president of the United States, happiness exploded from coast to coast. It burst from the United States and spread around the antiracist world. Davis was in the delirium of Oakland. People whom she did not know came up and hugged her as she walked the streets. She saw people singing to the heavens, and she saw people dancing in the streets. And the people Angela Davis saw and all the others around the world who were celebrating were not enraptured from the election of an individual; they were enraptured by the pride of the victory for Black people, by the success of millions of grassroots organizers, and because they had shown all those disbelievers, who had said that electing a Black president was impossible, to be wrong. Most of all, they were enraptured by the antiracist potential of a Black president.

But, like my mother says, there's not much payout for potential, is there? President Obama was a symbol. Yes, one of hope. One of progress. But also one of assimilationism. So much so that he was used to explain racism away. Used to absolve it. Obama fell in line with the likes of Lincoln, Du Bois, Washington, Douglass, and many others, who had flashes—true moments—of antiracist thought, but always seemed to assimilate under pressure. He rose to fame for calling out Bill Cosby for blaming Black people, then dived headfirst into assimilation shortly thereafter, critiquing Black people in the exact same ways. And just as with the Black leaders before him, the assimilation didn't work. Segregationists climbed out of every hateful hole and out from under every racist rock. They hated him, worked tirelessly to destroy and discredit him, and used him as a way to demean Black people. To ramp up racist absurdity and stereotypes, once again calling back to their favorite bigoted playlist, playing all the classic racist tunes—Black savage, Black dummy, Black do-nothing, Black be-nothing. Anything to smear President Obama and Black people in the media. Racist politicians and media personalities worked to figure out ways to tamp down the ego that they assumed came with a Black president.

And came with being Black in the time of a Black president.

And came with...being Black.

People started to die. People continued to die. Children's lives, ended at the hands of police officers and vigilantes who placed no value on Black humanity. Police officers and vigilantes who walk free. But, just like in other parts of America's racist history, antiracists push forth from the margins to fight back. Black President or not.

Alicia Garza, Patrisse Cullors, and Opal Tometi founded #BlackLivesMatter as a direct response to racist backlash in the form of police brutality. From the minds and hearts of these three Black women—two of whom are queer—this declaration of love intuitively signified that in order to truly be antiracists, we must also oppose all the sexism, homophobia, colorism, ethnocentrism, nativism, cultural prejudice, and class bias teeming and teaming with racism to harm so many Black lives. The antiracist declaration of the era quickly leaped from social media onto shouting signs and shouting mouths at antiracist protests across the country in 2014. These protesters rejected the racist declaration of six centuries: that Black lives don't matter. #BlackLivesMatter quickly transformed from an antiracist love declaration into an antiracist movement filled with young people operating in local BLM groups across the nation, often led by young Black women. Collectively, these activists were pressing against discrimination in all forms, in all areas of society, and from a myriad of vantage points. And in reaction to those who acted as if Black male lives mattered the most, antiracist feminists boldly demanded of America to #SayHerName, to shine light on the women who have also been affected by the hands and feet of racism. Perhaps they, the antiracist daughters of Davis, should be held up as symbols of hope, for taking potential and turning it into power. More important, perhaps we should all do the same.

AFTERWORD

How do you feel? I mean, I hope after reading this *not history* history book, you're left with some answers. I hope it's clear how the construct of race has always been used to gain and keep power, whether financially or politically. How it has always been used to create dynamics that separate us to keep us quiet. To keep the ball of White and rich privilege rolling. And that it's not woven into people as much as it's woven into policy that people adhere to and believe is truth.

Laws that have kept Black people from freedom, from voting, from education, from insurance, from housing, from government assistance, from health care, from shopping, from walking, from driving, from... breathing.

Laws that treat Black human beings like nothing. No, like animals.

Let's go with that. Animals. If we call a particular person a dog long enough, someone who is not like that person and who has more power than that person will believe it. Especially if we give the powerful person a leash and justify putting it around the oppressed person's neck. If we justify feeding them dog food. If we muzzle them when they bark, claiming that their barks, as well as their whines, are violent. If we clip their tail. Their ears. Punish them when they chew up the house, when they gnaw at the wooden door. And if we can convince the person with power that a child is a dog—if we present (fraudulent) pedigree papers—why would they even question humans (as dogs) being considered pets, being owned, trained, used, bred, and sold?

This is how racism works.

I mean, all it takes is the right kind of media to spark it. To spin it. At least, that's what history has shown us. Tell a certain story a certain way. Make a movie that paints you as the hero. Get enough people on your side to tell you you're right, and you're right. Even if you're wrong. And once you've been told you're right long enough, and once your being right has led you to a profitable and privileged life, you'd do anything to not be proved wrong. Even pretend human beings aren't human beings.

From Zurara to Harriet Beecher Stowe. Sojourner Truth to Audre Lorde. Ida B. Wells-Barnett to Zora Neale Hurston. Frederick Douglass to Marcus Garvey. Jack Johnson to Muhammad Ali. *Tarzan* to *Planet of the Apes*. Ma Rainey to Public Enemy. Langston Hughes to James Baldwin.

Cotton Mather

to Thomas Jefferson

to William Lloyd Garrison

to W. E. B. Du Bois

to Angela Davis

to Angela Davis

to Angela Davis,

leads back to the question of whether you, reader, want to be a segregationist (a hater), an assimilationist (a coward), or an antiracist (someone who truly loves).

Choice is yours.

Don't freak out.

Just breathe in. Inhale. Hold it. Now exhale slowly:

N O W.

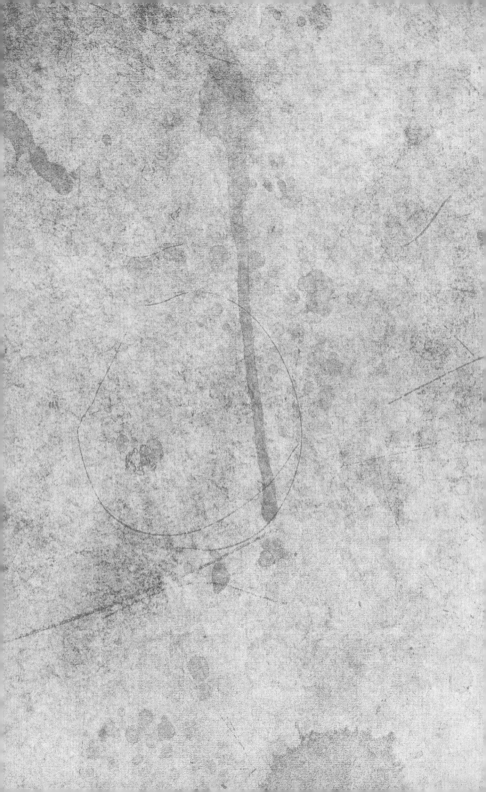

ACKNOWLEDGMENTS

THERE ARE SO MANY PEOPLE I NEED TO THANK, INCLUD-ing our editor, Lisa Yoskowitz at Little, Brown, and my agent, Elena Giovinazzo, both of whom believed I was capable of doing this. I'd like to thank my mother, who believes I'm capable of doing anything. And, of course, I'd like to thank Dr. Ibram X. Kendi. Your brilliance and diligence are to be praised. Thank you for being an example and for trusting me with such a special project. More important, thank you for this massive and ground-breaking contribution to our complex history. Your book is a new cornerstone in the American race conversation. Your voice is a new tuning fork.

But there is no one I'd like to thank more than all the young people. Those who have read this book (and are now reading it) and those who may never break the spine. All of you deserve thanks. All of you deserve acknowledgment. All of you deserve to know that you are in fact the antidote to anti-Blackness, xenophobia, homophobia, classism, sexism, and the other cancers that you have not caused but surely have the potential to cure.

You know how I know this? Because I'm one of the fortunate people who get to spend time with you. I've been in your schools, have walked the hallways with you. I've sat at your lunch tables and cracked jokes with you. I've popped into your libraries and community centers, from the suburbs to public-housing complexes. I've been to the alternative schools and the detention centers. From inner city to Iowa. And what I've learned is that you're far more open and empathetic than the generations before you. So much so, that your sensitivity is used as an insult, a slight against you. Your desire for a fair world is seen as a weakness. What I've learned is that your anger is global, because the world now sits in the palm of your hand. You have the ability to teleport, to scroll upon a war zone or a murder. To witness protest and revolution from cultures not your own but who share your frustration. Your refusal. Your fear.

But I have to warn you:

Scrolling will never be enough.

Reposting will never be enough.

Hashtagging will never be enough.

Because hatred has a way of convincing us that half love is whole. What I mean by that is we—all of us—have to fight against performance and lean into participation. We have to be participants. Active. We have to be more than audience members sitting comfortably in the stands of morality, shouting, "WRONG!" That's too easy. Instead, we must be players on the field, on the court, in our classrooms and communities, trying to *do* right. Because it takes a whole hand—both hands—to grab hold of hatred. Not just a texting thumb and a scrolling index finger.

But I have to warn you, again:

We can't attack a thing we don't know.

That's dangerous. And...foolish. It would be like trying to chop down a tree from the top of it. If we understand how the tree works, how the trunk and roots are where the power lies, and how gravity is on our side, we can attack it, each of us with small axes, and change the face of the forest.

So let's learn all there is to know about the tree of racism. The root. The fruit. The sap and trunk. The nests built over time, the changing leaves. That way, your generation can finally, actively chop it down.

Thank you, young people. I wish I could name you all. But I'd much rather you name yourselves.

Jason

I would like to acknowledge all the people I know and do not know who assisted and supported me in composing *Stamped from the Beginning*, which this book is based on. From my ever-loving family members and friends to my ever-supportive colleagues across academia and at American University, and to the countless thinkers, dead and alive, inside and outside academia, whose works on race have shaped my thinking and this history—I thank you. Without a doubt, this book is as much by you as it is by me.

I aimed to write a history book that could be devoured by as many people as possible—without shortchanging the serious complexities—because racist ideas and their history have affected all of us. But Jason Reynolds took his remix of *Stamped from the Beginning* to another level of accessibility and luster. I can't thank him enough for his willingness to produce this sophisticated remix that will impact generations of young and not so young people.

I would like to acknowledge my agent, Ayesha Pande,

who from the beginning was one of the major champions of *Stamped from the Beginning* and *Stamped: Racism, Antiracism, and You*. Ayesha, I do not take for granted that you believed in these books. And I must thank Little, Brown Books for Young Readers and our remarkable editor, Lisa Yoskowitz, who from the beginning clearly recognized the importance and potential impact of *Stamped*. To Katy O'Donnell at Bold Type Books, thank you again for working with me on *Stamped from the Beginning*. To Michelle Campbell, Jackie Engel, Jen Graham, Karina Granda, Siena Koncsol, Christie Michel, Michael Pietsch, Emilie Polster, Victoria Stapleton, Megan Tingley—to all the people involved in the production and marketing of this book, I cannot thank you enough.

I would like to give a special acknowledgment to my parents, Carol and Larry Rogers, and to my brothers, Akil and Macharia. Love is truly a verb, and I thank you for your love.

I saved one person, who was as excited as I was that Jason and I were working together on this book, for last—my wife, Sadiqa. Thank you, Sadiqa, and thank you, everyone, for everything.

Ibram

FURTHER READING

FOR FURTHER READING, CHECK OUT:

Complete Writings by Phillis Wheatley (Penguin
  Classics, 2001)
Narrative of the Life of Frederick Douglass by Frederick
  Douglass (Anti-Slavery Office, 1845; Signet
  Classics Edition, 2005)
Narrative of Sojourner Truth by Sojourner Truth
  (Printed for the Author, 1850; Penguin Classic
  Editions, 1998)
Their Eyes Were Watching God by Zora Neale Hurston
  (J. B. Lippincott, 1937; HarperCollins, 2000)
The Black Jacobins by C. L. R. James (Secker &
  Warburg, 1938)
Native Son by Richard Wright (Harper & Brothers,
  1940)

Montage of a Dream Deferred by Langston Hughes (Henry Holt, 1951)

Invisible Man by Ralph Ellison (Random House, 1952)

The Fire Next Time by James Baldwin (Dial Press, 1963)

The Autobiography of Malcolm X: As Told to Alex Haley by Malcolm X (Grove Press, 1965; Ballantine Books, 1992)

I Know Why the Caged Bird Sings by Maya Angelou (Random House, 1969)

The Bluest Eye by Toni Morrison (Holt, Rinehart and Winston, 1970)

The Dutchman by LeRoi Jones (Quill Editions, 1971)

The Color Purple by Alice Walker (Harcourt Brace Jovanovich, 1982)

Women, Race, and Class by Angela Y. Davis (Vintage Books, 1983)

Sister Outsider by Audre Lorde (Crossing Press, 1984)

For Colored Girls Who Have Considered Suicide/When the Rainbow Is Enuf by Ntozake Shange (Scribner, 1989)

Monster by Walter Dean Myers (HarperCollins, 1999)

The New Jim Crow by Michelle Alexander (The New Press, 2010)

Black Cool: One Thousand Streams of Blackness by Rebecca Walker (Soft Skull Press, 2012)

Long Division by Kiese Laymon (Agate Bolden, 2013)

Brown Girl Dreaming by Jacqueline Woodson (Putnam/ Nancy Paulsen Books, 2014)

How It Went Down by Kekla Magoon (Henry Holt, 2014)

All American Boys by Jason Reynolds and Brendan Kiely (Atheneum/Caitlyn Dlouhy Books, 2015)

Between the World and Me by Ta-Nehisi Coates (Spiegel & Grau, 2015)

March (Books 1–3) by John Lewis (Top Shelf Productions, 2016)

Stamped from the Beginning by Ibram X. Kendi (Bold Type Books, 2016)

The Fire This Time edited by Jesmyn Ward (Scribner, 2016)

Dear Martin by Nic Stone (Crown Books for Young Readers, 2017)

Long Way Down by Jason Reynolds (Atheneum/Caitlyn Dlouhy Books, 2017)

Miles Morales: Spider-Man (A Marvel YA Novel) by Jason Reynolds (Marvel Press, 2017)

The Hate U Give by Angie Thomas (Balzer + Bray, 2017)

Anger Is a Gift by Mark Oshiro (Tor Teen, 2018)

Barracoon by Zora Neale Hurston (Amistad, 2018)

Friday Black by Nana Kwame Adjei-Brenyah
  (Houghton Mifflin Harcourt, 2018)

Ghost Boys by Jewell Parker Rhodes (Little, Brown
  Books for Young Readers, 2018)

Black Enough edited by Ibi Zoboi (Balzer + Bray, 2019)

How to Be an Antiracist by Ibram X. Kendi (One World,
  2019)

Watch Us Rise by Renée Watson and Ellen Hagan
  (Bloomsbury, 2019)

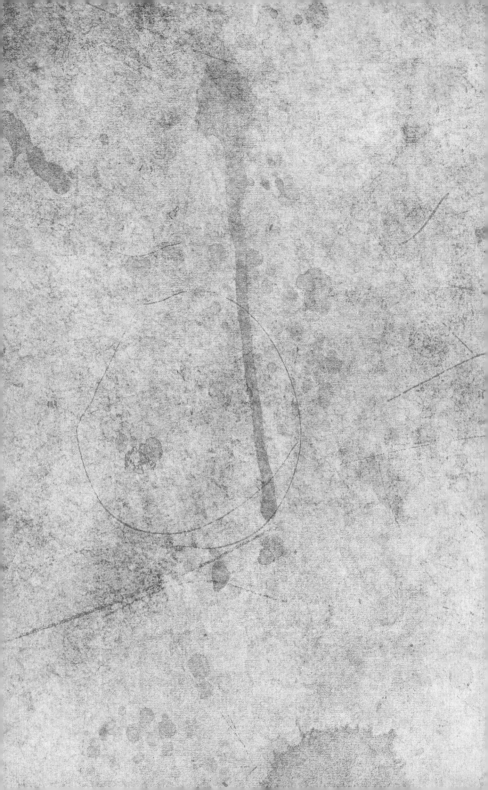

SOURCE NOTES

INTRODUCTION

xi Young Black males were *twenty-one times* more likely to be killed: Ryan Gabrielson, Ryann Grochowski Jones, and Eric Sagara, "Deadly Force, in Black and White," *ProPublica*, October 10, 2014; Rakesh Kochhar and Richard Fry, "Wealth Inequality Has Widened Along Racial, Ethnic Lines Since End of Great Recession," December 12, 2014, Pew Research Center, www.pewresearch.org/fact-tank/2014/12/12/racial -wealth-gaps-great-recession; Sabrina Tavernise, "Racial Disparities in Life Spans Narrow, but Persist," *New York Times*, July 18, 2013, www .nytimes.com/2013/07/18/health/racial-disparities-in-life-spans -narrow-but-persist.html.

xii Black people should make up somewhere close to 13 percent: Leah Sakala, "Breaking Down Mass Incarceration in the 2010 Census: State-by-State Incarceration Rates by Race/Ethnicity," *Prison Policy Initiative*, May 28, 2014, www.prisonpolicy.org/reports/rates.html; Matt Bruenig, "The Racial Wealth Gap," *American Prospect*, November 6, 2013, http://prospect.org/article/racial-wealth-gap.

xii Historically, there have been three groups involved: Ruth Benedict, *Race: Science and Politics* (New York: Modern Age Books, 1940); Ruth Benedict, *Race and Racism* (London: G. Routledge and Sons, 1942).

SECTION 1: 1415–1728

CHAPTER 1: The Story of the World's First Racist

6 He wrote the story, a biography of the life and slave trading of Prince Henry: P. E. Russell, *Prince Henry "the Navigator": A Life* (New Haven,

CT: Yale University Press, 2000), 6; Gomes Eanes de Zurara, Charles Raymond Beazley, and Edgar Prestage, *Chronicle of the Discovery and Conquest of Guinea*, 2 vols. (London: Printed for the Hakluyt Society, 1896), 1, 6, 7, 29.

7   Prince Henry's cut, like a finder's fee: 185 slaves: Hugh Thomas, *The Slave Trade: The Story of the Atlantic Slave Trade, 1440–1870* (New York: Simon and Schuster, 1997); Zurara et al., *Chronicle*, xx–xl; Russell, *Prince Henry "the Navigator,"* 246.

8   the primary source of knowledge on unknown Africa and African peoples: Zurara et al., *Chronicle*, lv–lviii; Francisco Bethencourt, *Racisms: From the Crusades to the Twentieth Century* (Princeton, NJ: Princeton University Press, 2013), 187.

8   Africanus echoed Zurara's sentiments of Africans: Leo Africanus, John Pory, and Robert Brown, *The History and Description of Africa*, 3 vols. (London: Hakluyt Society, 1896), 130, 187–190.

CHAPTER 2: Puritan Power

12   This actually came from Aristotle: Bethencourt, *Racisms*, 3, 13–15; David Goldenberg, "Racism, Color Symbolism, and Color Prejudice," in *The Origins of Racism in the West*, ed. Miriam Eliav-Feldon, Benjamin Isaac, and Joseph Ziegler (Cambridge, UK: Cambridge University Press, 2009), 88–92; Aristotle, edited and translated by Ernest Barker, *The Politics of Aristotle* (Oxford: Clarendon Press, 1946), 91253b; Peter Garnsey, *Ideas of Slavery from Aristotle to Augustine* (New York: Cambridge University Press, 1996), 114.

12   English travel writer George Best determined: Gary Taylor, *Buying Whiteness: Race, Culture, and Identity from Columbus to Hip Hop*, Signs of Race (New York: Palgrave Macmillan, 2005), 222–223; Joseph R. Washington, *Anti-Blackness in English Religion, 1500–1800* (New York: E. Mellen Press, 1984), 113–114.

13   the strange concept that…the relationship between slave and master was loving; William Perkins…argued that the slave was just part of a loving family unit: Everett H. Emerson, *John Cotton* (New York: Twayne, 1965), 18, 20, 37, 88, 98, 100, 108–109, 111, 131; Washington, *Anti-Blackness*, 174–182.

15   They landed in America after treacherous trips: Richard Mather, *Journal of Richard Mather: 1635, His Life and Death, 1670* (Boston: D. Clapp,

1850), 27–28; "Great New England Hurricane of 1635 Even Worse Than Thought," Associated Press, November 21, 2006.

15 Both men were ministers: Samuel Eliot Morison, *The Founding of Harvard College* (Cambridge, MA: Harvard University Press, 1935), 242–243; Richard Mather et al., *The Whole Booke of Psalmes Faithfully Translated into English Metre* (Cambridge, MA: S. Daye, 1640); John Cotton, *Spiritual Milk for Boston Babes in Either England* (Boston: S. G., for Hezekiah Usher, 1656); Christopher J. Lucas, *American Higher Education: A History*, 2nd ed. (New York: Palgrave Macmillan, 2006), 109–110; Frederick Rudolph, *Curriculum: A History of the American Undergraduate Course of Study Since 1636* (San Francisco: Jossey-Bass, 1977), 29–30.

16 Cotton and Mather were students of Aristotle; According to the Puritans, they were better than: Bethencourt, *Racisms*, 3, 13–15; Goldenberg, "Racism," 88–92; Aristotle, *Politics*, 91253b; Garnsey, *Ideas*, 114.

17 during the development of Harvard: Morison, *Founding*, 242–243; Mather et al., *The Whole Booke*; Cotton, *Spiritual Milk*; Lucas, *American Higher Education*, 109–110; Rudolph, *Curriculum*, 29–30.

18 was named America's first legislative leader: Jon Meacham, *Thomas Jefferson: The Art of Power* (New York: Random House, 2012), 5.

18 First thing he did was set the price of tobacco: Alden T. Vaughan, *Roots of American Racism: Essays on the Colonial Experience* (New York: Oxford University Press, 1995), 130–134.

18 the *San Juan Bautista* was hijacked: Tim Hashaw, *The Birth of Black America: The First African Americans and the Pursuit of Freedom at Jamestown* (New York: Carroll and Graf, 2007), xv–xvi.

18 slaves would cause a bit of conflict between the two: Edmund S. Morgan, *American Slavery, American Freedom: The Ordeal of Colonial Virginia* (New York: W. W. Norton, 1975), 348–351; Parke Rouse, *James Blair of Virginia* (Chapel Hill: University of North Carolina Press, 1971), 16–22, 25–26, 30, 37–38, 40, 43, 71–73, 145, 147–148; Albert J. Raboteau, *Slave Religion: The "Invisible Institution" in the Antebellum South* (New York: Oxford University Press, 1978), 100; Kenneth Silverman, *The Life and Times of Cotton Mather* (New York: Harper and Row, 1984), 241–242.

CHAPTER 3: A Different Adam

22 Notes on Baxter: Richard Baxter, *A Christian Directory* (London: Richard Edwards, 1825), 216–220.

22 Notes on Locke: R. S. Woolhouse, *Locke: A Biography* (Cambridge, UK: Cambridge University Press, 2007), 98, 276; Jeffrey Robert Young, "Introduction," in *Proslavery and Sectional Thought in the Early South, 1740–1829: An Anthology*, ed. Jeffrey Robert Young (Columbia: University of South Carolina Press, 2006), 18.

23 Mennonites in Germantown, Pennsylvania, rose up: Washington, *Anti-Blackness*, 460–461; Hildegard Binder-Johnson, "The Germantown Protest of 1688 Against Negro Slavery," *Pennsylvania Magazine of History and Biography* 65 (1941): 151; Katharine Gerbner, "'We Are Against the Traffik of Men-Body': The Germantown Quaker Protest of 1688 and the Origins of American Abolitionism," *Pennsylvania History: A Journal of Mid-Atlantic Studies* 74, no. 2 (2007): 159–166; Thomas, *Slave Trade*, 458; "William Edmundson," *The Friend: A Religious and Literary Journal* 7, no. 1 (1833): 5–6.

25 Native American and new (White) American beef had been brewing: Craig Steven Wilder, *Ebony & Ivy: Race, Slavery, and the Troubled History of America's Universities* (New York: Bloomsbury Press), 40.

26 Bacon was upset not about the race issue: Ronald T. Takaki, *A Different Mirror: A History of Multicultural America* (Boston: Little, Brown, 1993), 63–68; Anthony S. Parent, *Foul Means: The Formation of a Slave Society in Virginia, 1660–1740* (Chapel Hill: University of North Carolina Press, 2003), 126–127, 143–146; David R. Roediger, *How Race Survived U.S. History: From Settlement and Slavery to the Obama Phenomenon* (London: Verso, 2008), 19–20; Morgan, *American Slavery, American Freedom*, 252–270, 328–329.

CHAPTER 4: A Racist Wunderkind

29 they had a grandson: Washington, *Anti-Blackness*, 455–456; Lorenzo J. Greene, *The Negro in Colonial New England, 1620–1776* (New York: Columbia University Press, 1942), 275; Young, "Introduction," 19–21; Brycchan Carey, *From Peace to Freedom: Quaker Rhetoric and the Birth of American Antislavery, 1657–1761* (New Haven, CT: Yale University Press, 2012), 7–8.

30 By the time Cotton Mather heard about Bacon's rebellion: Silverman,

Life and Times of Cotton Mather; Tony Williams, *The Pox and the Covenant: Mather, Franklin, and the Epidemic That Changed America's Destiny* (Naperville, IL: Sourcebooks, 2010), 34.

30 He knew he was special: Robert Middlekauff, *The Mathers: Three Generations of Puritan Intellectuals, 1596–1728* (New York: Oxford University Press, 1971), 198–199; Ralph Philip Boas and Louise Schutz Boas, *Cotton Mather: Keeper of the Puritan Conscience* (Hamden, CT: Archon Books, 1964), 27–31.

30 Because he was so insecure about his speech impediment: Greene, *The Negro in Colonial New England*, 237; Silverman, *Life and Times of Cotton Mather*, 31, 36–37, 159–160.

32 Mather wrote a book: Philip Jenkins, *Intimate Enemies: Moral Panics in Contemporary Great Britain* (New York: Aldine de Gruyter, 1992), 3–5; Silverman, *Life and Times of Cotton Mather*, 84–85.

32 no one poured gasoline on the witchy fire like a minister: Edward J. Blum and Paul Harvey, *The Color of Christ: The Son of God & the Saga of Race in America* (Chapel Hill: University of North Carolina Press, 2012), 20–21, 27, 40–41; Silverman, *Life and Times of Cotton Mather*, 88–89.

33 turned attention away from the political and onto the religious: Charles Wentworth Upham, *Salem Witchcraft; with an Account of Salem Village, a History of Opinions on Witchcraft and Kindred Subjects*, vol. 1 (Boston: Wiggin and Lunt, 1867), 411–412; Blum and Harvey, *The Color of Christ*, 27–28; Boas and Boas, *Cotton Mather*, 109–110.

33 Massachusetts authorities apologized: Silverman, *Life and Times of Cotton Mather*, 83–120; Thomas N. Ingersoll, "'Riches and Honour Were Rejected by Them as Loathsome Vomit': The Fear of Leveling in New England," in *Inequality in Early America*, ed. Carla Gardina Pestana and Sharon Vineberg Salinger (Hanover, NH: University Press of New England, 1999), 46–54.

34 Mather's ideas and writings spread: Cotton Mather, *Diary of Cotton Mather, 1681–1724*, 2 vols., vol. 1 (Boston: The Society, 1911), 226–229; Silverman, *Life and Times of Cotton Mather*, 262–263; Parent, *Foul Means*, 86–89.

34 As the population of enslaved people grew: Parent, *Foul Means*, 120–123; Morgan, *American Slavery, American Freedom*, 330–344; Greene, *The Negro in Colonial New England*, 171.

35 Enslavers became more open: Greene, *The Negro in Colonial New England*, 275–276; Jon Sensbach, "Slaves to Intolerance: African American Christianity and Religious Freedom in Early America," in *The First Prejudice: Religious Tolerance and Intolerance in Early America*, ed. Chris Beneke and Christopher S. Grenda (Philadelphia: University of Pennsylvania Press, 2011), 208–209; Kenneth P. Minkema, "Jonathan Edwards's Defense of Slavery," *Massachusetts Historical Review* 4 (2002): 23, 24, 40; Francis D. Adams and Barry Sanders, *Alienable Rights: The Exclusion of African Americans in a White Man's Land, 1619–2000* (New York: HarperCollins, 2003), 40–41.

36 Cotton Mather continued to age: Silverman, *Life and Times of Cotton Mather*, 372–419.

SECTION 2: 1743–1826

CHAPTER 5: Proof in the Poetry

42 Franklin started a club called the American Philosophical Society: Benjamin Franklin, "A Proposal for Promoting Useful Knowledge Among the British Plantations in America," *Transactions of the Literary and Philosophical Society of New York* 1, no. 1 (1815): 89–90.

42 in a house where Native Americans were houseguests: Thomas Jefferson, "To John Adams," in *The Writings of Thomas Jefferson*, ed. H. A. Washington (Washington, DC: Taylor and Maury, 1854), 61.

43 when his African "friends" started telling him about the horrors: Thomas Jefferson, *Notes on the State of Virginia* (London: J. Stockdale, 1787), 271.

44 Phillis Wheatley was under a microscope: Henry Louis Gates, *The Trials of Phillis Wheatley: America's First Black Poet and Her Encounters with the Founding Fathers* (New York: Basic Civitas, 2010), 14.

44 a captive brought over on a ship: Vincent Carretta, *Phillis Wheatley: Biography of a Genius in Bondage* (Athens: University of Georgia Press, 2011), 4–5, 7–8, 12–14; Kathrynn Seidler Engberg, *The Right to Write: The Literary Politics of Anne Bradstreet and Phillis Wheatley* (Lanham, MD: University Press of America, 2010), 35–36.

44 because she was a "daughter": Carretta, *Phillis Wheatley*, 1–17, 37–38.

45 got eighteen of the smartest men in America together: Gates, *The Trials of Phillis Wheatley*, 14.

47 Wheatley was over in London being trotted around like a superstar: Carretta, *Phillis Wheatley*, 91, 95–98; Gates, *Trials of Phillis Wheatley*, 33–34; Phillis Wheatley, *Poems on Various Subjects, Religious and Moral* (London: A. Bell, 1773).

CHAPTER 8: Jefferson's Notes

56 sat down to pen the Declaration of Independence: Meacham, *Thomas Jefferson*, 103.

56 they were running away from plantations all over the South: Jacqueline Jones, *A Dreadful Deceit: The Myth of Race from the Colonial Era to Obama's America* (New York: Basic Books, 2013), 64.

57 slavery was a "cruel war against human nature": Joseph J. Ellis, *American Sphinx: The Character of Thomas Jefferson* (New York: Alfred A. Knopf, 1997), 27–71; Meacham, *Thomas Jefferson*, 106.

57 he expressed his real thoughts on Black people: Jefferson, *Notes on the State of Virginia*, 229.

58 intelligent blacksmiths, shoemakers, bricklayers: Herbert Aptheker, *Anti-Racism in U.S. History: The First Two Hundred Years* (New York: Greenwood Press, 1992), 47–48.

58 He ran. To France: Meacham, *Thomas Jefferson*, xxvi, 144, 146, 175, 180.

59 Jefferson was telling his slaves to work harder: Adams and Sanders, *Alienable Rights*, 88–89; Meacham, *Thomas Jefferson*, 188–189; Thomas Jefferson, "To Brissot de Warville, February 11, 1788," in *The Papers of Thomas Jefferson*, 12:577–578.

60 Every five slaves equaled three humans: David O. Stewart, *The Summer of 1787: The Men Who Invented the Constitution* (New York: Simon and Schuster, 2007), 68–81.

61 enslaved Africans in Haiti rose up against French rule: Meacham, *Thomas Jefferson*, 231–235, 239, 241, 249, 254.

CHAPTER 9: Uplift Suasion

65 abolitionists urged the newly freed people: Leon F. Litwack, *North of Slavery: The Negro in the Free States, 1790–1860* (Chicago: University of Chicago Press, 1961), 18–19; Joanne Pope Melish, "The 'Condition' Debate and Racial Discourse in the Antebellum North," *Journal of the Early Republic* 19 (1999), 651–657, 661–665.

CHAPTER 10: The Great Contradictor

69 The Prossers were planning a slave rebellion: Herbert Aptheker, *American Negro Slave Revolts* (New York: International Publishers, 1963), 222–223.

70 up from the soil of slavery sprouted new racist ideas: Larry E. Tise, *Proslavery: A History of the Defense of Slavery in America, 1701–1840* (Athens: University of Georgia Press, 1987), 58.

71 Charles Fenton Mercer, and an antislavery clergyman: Charles Fenton Mercer, *An Exposition of the Weakness and Inefficiency of the Government of the United States of North America* (n.p., 1845), 173, 284.

71 Black people didn't want to go "back": Scott L. Malcomson, *One Drop of Blood: The American Misadventure of Race* (New York: Farrar, Straus, and Giroux, 2000), 191; Robert Finley, "Thoughts on the Colonization of Free Blacks," *African Repository and Colonial Journal* 9 (1834), 332–334.

72 did nothing to stop domestic slavery: Angela Y. Davis, *Women, Race & Class* (New York: Vintage Books, 1983), 7; Thomas, *Slave Trade*, 551–552, 568–572; Peter Kolchin, *American Slavery, 1619–1877*, rev. ed. (New York: Hill and Wang, 2003), 93–95; Thomas Jefferson, "To John W. Eppes, June 30, 1820," in *Thomas Jefferson's Farm Book: With Commentary and Relevant Extracts from Other Writings*, ed. Edwin Morris Betts (Princeton, NJ: Princeton University Press, 1953), 46.

75 almost as if he'd be sending Black people home from camp: Thomas Jefferson to Jared Sparks Monticello, February 4, 1824, *The Letters of Thomas Jefferson, 1743–1826*, American History, www.let.rug.nl/usa/presidents/thomas-jefferson/letters-of-thomas-jefferson/jefl276.php.

77 so sick he was unable to attend the fiftieth anniversary: Meacham, *Thomas Jefferson*, 488.

77 Jefferson seemed to be fighting to stay alive: Silvio A. Bedini, *Thomas Jefferson: Statesman of Science* (New York: Macmillan, 1990), 478–480; Meacham, *Thomas Jefferson*, 48, 492–496.

SECTION 3: 1826–1879

CHAPTER 11: Mass Communication for Mass Emancipation

85 those legacies were deeply entwined with slavery: Wilder, *Ebony & Ivy*, 255, 256, 259, 265–266.

85 Garrison had gone even further to the side of abolitionism: Henry Mayer, *All on Fire: William Lloyd Garrison and the Abolition of Slavery* (New York: St. Martin's Press, 1998), 62–68.

87 In his first editorial piece, Garrison changed perspectives: William Lloyd Garrison, "To the Public," *Liberator*, January 1, 1831.

88 That he was called upon by God to plan and execute a massive crusade: Aptheker, *American Negro Slave Revolts*, 293–295, 300–307; Blum and Harvey, *The Color of Christ*, 123; Nat Turner and Thomas R. Gray, *The Confessions of Nat Turner* (Richmond: T. R. Gray, 1832), 9–10.

88 members decided to rely on the new technology of mass printing: Mayer, *All on Fire*, 195; Russel B. Nye, *William Lloyd Garrison and the Humanitarian Reformers*, Library of American Biography (Boston: Little, Brown, 1955), 81–82.

CHAPTER 12: Uncle Tom

91 father of American anthropology, who was measuring the skulls: Samuel George Morton, *Crania Americana* (Philadelphia: J. Dobson, 1839), 1–7.

92 free blacks were insane: Edward Jarvis, "Statistics of Insanity in the United States," *Boston Medical and Surgical Journal* 27, no. 7 (1842): 116–121.

92 there was a "White" Egypt that had Black slaves: William Ragan Stanton, *The Leopard's Spots: Scientific Attitudes toward Race in America, 1815–59* (Chicago: University of Chicago Press, 1960), 45–53, 60–65; George M. Fredrickson, *The Black Image in the White Mind: The Debate on Afro-American Character and Destiny, 1817–1914* (Middletown, CT: Wesleyan University Press, 1987), 74–75; H. Shelton Smith, *In His Image, But…: Racism in Southern Religion, 1780–1910* (Durham, NC: Duke University Press, 1972), 144; Litwack, *North of Slavery*, 46.

93 in America proslavery politicians—now with Texas as a slave state: Juan González and Joseph Torres, *News for All the People: The Epic Story of Race and the American Media* (London: Verso, 2011), 118–119.

CHAPTER 13: Complicated Abe

100 if labor was free, what exactly were poor White people expected to do: Hinton Rowan Helper, *The Impending Crisis of the South: How to Meet It* (New York: Burdick Brothers, 1857), 184.

101 Garrison, though critical of Lincoln, kept his critiques to himself: Mayer, *All on Fire*, 474–477.

102 started with South Carolina. They left the Union: "Declaration of the Immediate Causes Which Induce and Justify Secession of South Carolina from the Federal Union," The Avalon Project: Documents in Law, History and Diplomacy, Lillian Goldman Law Library, Yale Law School, http://avalon.law.yale.edu/19th_century/csa_scarsec.asp; Roediger, *How Race Survived U.S. History*, 70–71; Eric Foner, *Reconstruction: America's Unfinished Revolution, 1863–1877* (New York: Perennial Classics, 2002), 25; Eric Foner, *The Fiery Trial: Abraham Lincoln and American Slavery* (New York: W. W. Norton, 2010), 146–147; Myron O. Stachiw, "'For the Sake of Commerce': Slavery, Antislavery, and Northern Industry," in *The Meaning of Slavery in the North*, ed. David Roediger and Martin H. Blatt (New York: Garland, 1998), 33–35.

103 Union soldiers were enforcing the Fugitive Slave Act: William C. Davis, *Look Away!: A History of the Confederate States of America* (New York: Free Press, 2002), 142–143.

104 "All persons held as slaves within any state": Abraham Lincoln, "Preliminary Emancipation Proclamation," September 22, 1862, National Archives and Records Administration, www.archives.gov/exhibits /american_originals_iv/sections/transcript_preliminary_emancipation .html.

104 four hundred thousand black people had escaped their plantations: Foner, *Fiery Trial*, 238–247; Paul D. Escott, *"What Shall We Do with the Negro?" Lincoln, White Racism, and Civil War America* (Charlottesville: University of Virginia Press, 2009), 62–63.

105 What good was it to be free if they had nowhere to go: "Account of a Meeting of Black Religious Leaders in Savannah, Georgia, with the Secretary of War and the Commander of the Military Division of the Mississippi," in *Freedom: A Documentary History of Emancipation, 1861–1867*, series 1, vol. 3, ed. Ira Berlin et al. (New York: Cambridge University Press, 1982), 334–335.

105 They'd run up to him in the street: Foner, *Reconstruction*, 73.

105 that Blacks (the intelligent ones) should have the right to vote: Foner, *Reconstruction*, 31, 67–68; Foner, *Fiery Trial*, 330–331.

105 he was shot in the back of the head: Terry Alford, *Fortune's Fool: The Life of John Wilkes Booth* (New York: Oxford University Press, 2015), 257.

CHAPTER 14: Garrison's Last Stand

107 his job as an abolitionist was done: Foner, *Reconstruction*, 67; Adams and Sanders, *Alienable Rights*, 196–197; Hans L. Trefousse, *Andrew Johnson: A Biography* (New York: W. W. Norton, 1989), 183; Clifton R. Hall, *Andrew Johnson: Military Governor of Tennessee* (Princeton, NJ: Princeton University Press, 1916), 102.

110 no one could be prohibited from voting: Foner, *Reconstruction*, 446–447; Fredrickson, *The Black Image in the White Mind*, 185–186; C. Vann Woodward, *American Counterpoint: Slavery and Racism in the North-South Dialogue* (Boston: Little, Brown, 1971), 177–179.

110 Black people from Boston to Richmond: Forrest G. Wood, *Black Scare: The Racist Response to Emancipation and Reconstruction* (Berkeley: University of California Press, 1968), 102.

112 He'd wanted immediate emancipation: Adams and Sanders, *Alienable Rights*, 228; Foner, *Reconstruction*, 598–602; Mayer, *All on Fire*, 624–626.

SECTION 4: 1868–1963

CHAPTER 15: Battle of the Black Brains

118 Willie was hit with his first racial experience: David Levering Lewis, *W. E. B. Du Bois: Biography of a Race, 1868–1919* (New York: Henry Holt, 1993), 11–37.

119 sent young Willie to Fisk University: Lewis, *W. E. B. Du Bois, 1868–1919*, 51–76.

119 he gave credit to Jefferson Davis: Lewis, *W. E. B. Du Bois, 1868–1919*, 100–102.

120 mulattoes were practically the same as any White man: Albert Bushnell Hart, *The Southern South* (New York: D. Appleton, 1910), 99–105, 134; Lewis, *W. E. B. Du Bois, 1868–1919*, 111–113.

120 Du Bois wasn't the only Black man: Giddings, *When and Where I Enter*, 18; Ida B. Wells, *Southern Horrors: Lynch Law in All Its Phases* (New York: New York Age, 1892), www.gutenberg.org/files/14975/14975-h/14975-h.htm; Adams and Sanders, *Alienable Rights*, 231–232.

121 she found that from a sampling of 728 lynching reports: Giddings,

When and Where I Enter, 18; Ida B. Wells, *Southern Horrors*; Adams and Sanders, *Alienable Rights*, 231–232.

122 For Washington's private civil rights activism, see David H. Jackson, *Booker T. Washington and the Struggle Against White Supremacy: The Southern Educational Tours, 1908–1912* (New York: Palgrave Macmillan, 2008); David H. Jackson, *A Chief Lieutenant of the Tuskegee Machine: Charles Banks of Mississippi* (Gainesville: University Press of Florida, 2002).

123 White savior stories—were becoming a fixture in American media: Booker T. Washington, *Up from Slavery: An Autobiography* (New York: Doubleday, Page, 1901).

124 Du Bois introduced the idea of double consciousness: Aptheker, *Anti-Racism in U.S. History*, 25; W. E. B. Du Bois, *The Souls of Black Folk: Essays and Sketches* (Chicago: A. C. McClurg, 1903), 11–12.

124 one in every ten, he believed, were worthy of the job: Du Bois, *The Souls of Black Folk*, 53.

125 drawing similarities between the way his people were mistreated in Germany: Sander Gilman, *Jewish Frontiers: Essays on Bodies, Histories, and Identities* (New York: Palgrave Macmillan, 2003), 89.

126 an African history—wasn't one of inferiority: Michael Yudell, *Race Unmasked: Biology and Race in the Twentieth Century* (New York: Columbia University Press, 2014), 48–49; W. E. B. Du Bois, *Black Folk Then and Now: An Essay in the History and Sociology of the Negro Race* (New York: Henry Holt, 1939), vii.

126 One hundred sixty-seven soldiers, to be exact: Lewis, *W. E. B. Du Bois, 1868–1919*, 331–333; Theodore Roosevelt, "Sixth Annual Message," December 3, 1906, at Gerhard Peters and John T. Woolley, American Presidency Project, www.presidency.ucsb.edu/ws/?pid=29547.

127 Washington also had to feel the wrath: Lewis, *W. E. B. Du Bois, 1868–1919*, 332.

CHAPTER 16: Jack Johnson vs. Tarzan

132 They arrested him on trumped-up charges: John Gilbert, *Knuckles and Gloves* (London: W. Collins Sons, 1922), 45; González and Torres, *News for All the People*, 209–211; Geoffrey C. Ward, *Unforgivable*

Blackness: The Rise and Fall of Jack Johnson (New York: Alfred A. Knopf, 2004), 115–116.

133 He became a cultural phenomenon: Curtis A. Keim, *Mistaking Africa: Curiosities and Inventions of the American Mind*, 3rd ed. (Boulder: Westview Press, 2014), 48; Emily S. Rosenberg, *Financial Missionaries to the World: The Politics and Culture of Dollar Diplomacy, 1900–1930* (Durham, NC: Duke University Press, 2003), 201–203.

CHAPTER 18: The Mission Is in the Name

140 Who do you think sold more books: W. E. B. Du Bois, *The Autobiography of W. E. B. Du Bois: A Soliloquy on Viewing My Life from the Last Decade of Its First Century* (New York: International Publishers, 1968), 227–229.

140 he was confused about whether the NAACP was a Black organization: David Levering Lewis, *W. E. B. Du Bois: The Fight for Equality and the American Century, 1919–1963* (New York: Henry Holt, 1993), 50–55.

142 being treated decently overseas would embolden Black soldiers: Ira Katznelson, *When Affirmative Action Was White: An Untold History of Racial Inequality in Twentieth-Century America* (New York: W. W. Norton, 2005), 84–86.

143 in 1919, when many of those soldiers came home: Katznelson, *When Affirmative Action Was White*, 84–86.

143 1919 was the bloodiest summer: Cameron McWhirter, *Red Summer: The Summer of 1919 and the Awakening of Black America* (New York: Henry Holt, 2011), 10, 12–17, 56–59.

144 one of the most revolutionary things he did in the collection: W. E. B. Du Bois, *Darkwater: Voices from Within the Veil* (New York: Harcourt, Brace, and Howe, 1920), 166, 168, 185–186.

144 acted like he was a better Black person: Lewis, *W. E. B. Du Bois, 1919–1963*, 20–23.

144 if you weren't him—light-skinned, hyper-educated: Kathy Russell-Cole, Midge Wilson, and Ronald E. Hall, *The Color Complex: The Politics of Skin Color Among African Americans* (New York: Harcourt, Brace, Jovanovich, 1992), 26, 30–32; Giddings, *When and Where I Enter*, 178; Lewis, *W. E. B. Du Bois, 1919–1963*, 66–71.

145 charged him with mail fraud: Lewis, *W. E. B. Du Bois, 1919–1963*, 77–84, 118–128, 148–152.

CHAPTER 19: Can't Sing and Dance and Write It Away

147 he'd meet many of the young Black artists: Lewis, *W. E. B. Dubois, 1919–1963*, 153–159, 161–166; Alain Locke, "The New Negro," in *The New Negro: Voices of the Harlem Renaissance*, ed. Alain Locke (New York: Simon and Schuster, 1992), 15.

148 a resistant group of artists that emerged in 1926: Valerie Boyd, *Wrapped in Rainbows: The Life of Zora Neale Hurston* (New York: Simon and Schuster, 1997), 116–119; Wallace Thurman, *The Blacker the Berry* (New York: Simon and Schuster, 1996).

148 it was okay to be a Black artist without having to feel insecurity: Langston Hughes, "The Negro Artist and the Racial Mountain," *The Nation*, June 1926.

149 innocent White people were tortured: Claude G. Bowers, *The Tragic Era: The Revolution After Lincoln* (Cambridge, MA: Riverside, 1929), vi.

150 Reconstruction was stifled: Lewis, *W. E. B. Du Bois, 1919–1963*, 320–324; W. E. B. Du Bois, *Black Reconstruction in America: An Essay Towards a History of the Part Which Black Folk Played in the Attempt to Reconstruct Democracy in America, 1860–1880* (New York: Atheneum, 1971), 700, 725; David R. Roediger, *The Wages of Whiteness: Race and the Making of the American Working Class*, rev. ed. (London: Verso, 2007).

151 But in 1933, Du Bois wanted nothing to do with this method: Lewis, *W. E. B. Du Bois, 1919–1963*, 256–265, 299–301, 306–311.

151 critiquing Black colleges for having White-centered curriculums: Lewis, *W. E. B. Du Bois, 1919–1963*, 295–297, 300–314; James D. Anderson, *The Education of Blacks in the South, 1860–1935* (Chapel Hill: University of North Carolina Press, 1988), 276–277; Carter G. Woodson, *The Miseducation of the Negro* (Mineola, NY: Dover, 2005), 55.

152 there is a place, maybe even an importance, to a voluntary nondiscriminatory separation: W. E. B. Du Bois, "On Being Ashamed," *The Crisis*, September 1933; W. E. B. Du Bois, "Pan-Africa and New Racial Philosophy," *The Crisis*, November 1933; W. E. B. Du Bois, "Segregation," *The Crisis*, January 1934.

CHAPTER 20: Home Is Where the Hatred Is

156 These delegates did not make the politically racist request: Lewis, *W. E. B. Du Bois, 1919–1963*, 510–515.

157 that race problem was starting to affect its relationships: Robert L. Fleeger, "Theodore G. Bilbo and the Decline of Public Racism, 1938–1947," *Journal of Mississippi History* 68, no. 1 (2006), 2–3.

157 On February 2, 1948, Truman urged Congress: Harry S. Truman, "Special Message to the Congress on Civil Rights," February 2, 1948, at Gerhard Peters and John T. Woolley, The American Presidency Project, www .presidency.ucsb.edu/ws/?pid=13006; Robert A. Caro, *Means of Ascent: The Years of Lyndon Johnson*, vol. 2 (New York: Vintage, 1990), 125; Francis Njubi Nesbitt, *Race for Sanctions: African Americans Against Apartheid, 1946–1994* (Bloomington: Indiana University Press, 2004), 9–10.

158 This brought on the open housing movement: Thomas J. Sugrue, *The Origins of the Urban Crisis: Race and Inequality in Postwar Detroit*, Princeton Studies in American Politics (Princeton, NJ: Princeton University Press, 1996), 181–258; Douglas S. Massey and Nancy A. Denton, *American Apartheid: Segregation and the Making of the Underclass* (Cambridge, MA: Harvard University Press, 1993), 49–51.

159 racial segregation in public schools was unconstitutional: *Brown v. Board of Education of Topeka*, 347 U.S. 483 (1954), https://supreme.justia .com/cases/federal/us/347/483/case.html#T10.

160 students were staging sit-ins: Lewis, *W. E. B. Du Bois, 1919–1963*, 566.

161 *To Kill a Mockingbird* was basically the *Uncle Tom's Cabin*: Isaac Saney, "The Case Against *To Kill a Mockingbird*," *Race & Class* 45, no. 1 (2003): 99–110.

163 "Today we are committed to a worldwide struggle": Mary L. Dudziak, *Cold War Civil Rights: Race and the Image of American Democracy* (Princeton, NJ: Princeton University Press, 2000), 169–187.

164 W. E. B. Du Bois had died: Dudziak, *Cold War Civil Rights*, 187–200, 216–219; Du Bois, *W. E. B. Du Bois, 1868–1919*, 2.

SECTION 5: 1963–TODAY

CHAPTER 21: When Death Comes

169 She knew these names: Angela Y. Davis, *Angela Davis: An Autobiography* (New York: International Publishers, 1988), 128–131.

170 she would never—despite the pressure—desire to be White: Davis, *Autobiography*, 77–99.

170 White people who couldn't see that they weren't the standard: Davis, *Autobiography*, 101–112.

171 an inferiority complex forced on them: Davis, *Autobiography*, 117–127.

172 He launched an investigation: John F. Kennedy, "Statement by the President on the Sunday Bombing in Birmingham," September 16, 1963, Gerhard Peters and John T. Woolley, The American Presidency Project, www.presidency.ucsb.edu/ws/?pid=9410.

172 the civil rights bill that Kennedy had been working on: Lyndon B. Johnson, "Address to a Joint Session of Congress," November 27, 1963, *Public Papers of the Presidents of the United States: Lyndon B. Johnson, 1963–64*, vol. 1, entry 11 (Washington, DC: US Government Printing Office, 1965), 8–10.

173 Who was going to make sure the laws would be followed: Dudziak, *Cold War Civil Rights*, 208–214, 219–231; Malcolm X, "Appeal to African Heads of State," in *Malcolm X Speaks: Selected Speeches and Statements*, ed. George Breitman (New York: Grove Press, 1965), 76.

174 everyone—the North and the South—hated Black people: Dan T. Carter, *The Politics of Rage: George Wallace, the Origins of the New Conservatism, and the Transformation of American Politics* (Baton Rouge: Louisiana State University Press, 2000), 344.

174 government assistance, which White people had been receiving: Adams and Sanders, *Alienable Rights*, 287–291; Barry M. Goldwater, *The Conscience of a Conservative* (Washington, DC: Regnery, 1994), 67.

175 What leverage did he grant the SNCC and MFDP: Chana Kai Lee, *For Freedom's Sake: The Life of Fannie Lou Hamer*, Women in American History (Urbana: University of Illinois Press, 1999), 89, 99; Cleveland Sellers and Robert L. Terrell, *The River of No Return: The Autobiography of a Black Militant and the Life and Death of SNCC* (Jackson: University Press of Mississippi, 1990), 111.

176 When James Baldwin; When Dr. Martin Luther King: "Baldwin Blames White Supremacy," *New York Post*, February 22, 1965; Telegram from Martin Luther King Jr. to Betty al-Shabazz, February 26, 1965, The Martin Luther King Jr. Research and Education Institute, Stanford University, http://kingencyclopedia.stanford.edu/encyclopedia/documentsentry/telegram_from_martin_luther_king_jr_to_betty_al_shabazz/.

176 "Malcolm X's life was strangely": "Malcolm X," editorial, *New York Times*, February 22, 1965.

177 Malcolm X stamped that he was for truth: Eliot Fremont-Smith, "An Eloquent Testament," *New York Times*, November 5, 1965; Malcolm X and Alex Haley, *The Autobiography of Malcolm X* (New York: Ballantine, 1999).

177 the Voting Rights Act would become the most effective piece of antiracist legislation: US House of Representatives, "Voting Rights Act of 1965," House Report 439, 89th Cong., 1st sess. (Washington, DC: US Government Printing Office, 1965), 3.

CHAPTER 22: Black Power

180 the racist role of language symbolism: Davis, *Autobiography*, 133–139; Russell-Cole et al. *The Color Complex*, 59–61.

180 *Black* was for the antiracist: Ayana D. Byrd and Lori L. Tharps, *Hair Story: Untangling the Roots of Black Hair in America* (New York: St. Martin's Press, 2001).

181 "What we gonna start saying now is Black Power!": Peniel E. Joseph, *Waiting 'Til the Midnight Hour: A Narrative History of Black Power in America* (New York: Henry Holt, 2006), 141–142.

183 The Ten-Point Platform: Joshua Bloom and Waldo E. Martin, *Black Against Empire: The History and Politics of the Black Panther Party* (Berkeley: University of California Press, 2013), 70–73.

184 ramped up the Black Power movement: "New Black Consciousness Takes Over College Campus," *Chicago Defender*, December 4, 1967.

188 to introduce Black Studies departments: Ibram H. Rogers, *The Black Campus Movement: Black Students and the Racial Reconstitution of Higher Education, 1965–1972* (New York: Palgrave Macmillan, 2012), 114; Hillel Black, *The American Schoolbook* (New York: Morrow, 1967), 106; Joseph Moreau, *Schoolbook Nation: Conflicts over American History Textbooks from the Civil War to the Present* (Ann Arbor: University of Michigan Press, 2003).

189 working on the campaign for the first Black woman to run for the US presidency: Davis, *Autobiography*, 180–191.

CHAPTER 23: Murder Was the Case

192 without ever actually saying "Black people": Dan T. Carter, *From George Wallace to Newt Gingrich: Race in the Conservative Counterrevolution*

(Baton Rouge: Louisiana State University Press, 1996), 27; John Ehrlichman, *Witness to Power: The Nixon Years* (New York: Simon and Schuster, 1982), 223.

192 historians have named it: the "southern strategy": Carter, *From George Wallace to Newt Gingrich*, 27; Ehrlichman, *Witness to Power*, 223.

193 she was part of the Communist Party: Davis, *Autobiography*, 216–223; Earl Ofari Hutchinson, *Betrayed: A History of Presidential Failure to Protect Black Lives* (Boulder: Westview Press, 1996), 145–149.

193 were accused of murdering a prison guard: Davis, *Autobiography*, 250–255, 263–266.

196 Not free in her own mind: Davis, *Autobiography*, 359.

197 Black masculinity was what was frightening to White men: Charles Herbert Stember, *Sexual Racism: The Emotional Barrier to an Integrated Society* (New York: Elsevier, 1976).

198 from the perspective of being Black and lesbian: Audre Lorde, "Age, Race, Class, and Sex: Women Redefining Difference," in *Sister Outsider: Essays and Speeches*, ed. Audre Lorde (Berkeley, CA: Crossing Press, 2007), 115.

198 Ntozake Shange used her creative, antiracist energy: Salamishah Tillet, "Black Feminism, Tyler Perry Style," *The Root*, November 11, 2010, www.theroot.com/articles/culture/2010/11/a_feminist_analysis_of _tyler_perrys_for_colored_girls.html.

200 Rocky symbolized the pride of White supremacist masculinity's refusal to be knocked out: Ed Guerrero, *Framing Blackness: The African American Image in Film* (Philadelphia: Temple University Press, 1993), 113–138.

CHAPTER 24: What War on Drugs?

204 only 2 percent of Americans viewed drugs as America's most pressing problem: Michael K. Brown et al, *Whitewashing Race: The Myth of a Color-Blind Society* (Berkeley: University of California Press, 2003), 136–137; Michelle Alexander, *The New Jim Crow: Mass Incarceration in the Age of Colorblindness* (New York: New Press, 2010), 5–7, 49; Julian Roberts, "Public Opinion, Crime, and Criminal Justice," in *Crime and Justice: A Review of Research*, vol. 16, ed. Michael Tonry (Chicago: University of Chicago Press, 1992); Ronald Reagan, "Remarks on Signing

Executive Order 12368, Concerning Federal Drug Abuse Policy Functions," June 24, 1982, Gerhard Peters and John T. Woolley, The American Presidency Project, www.presidency.ucsb.edu/ws/?pid=42671.

204 Reagan doubled down on the War on Drugs: "Reagan Signs Anti-Drug Measure; Hopes for 'Drug-Free Generation,'" *New York Times*, October 28, 1968, www.nytimes.com/1986/10/28/us/reagan-signs-anti-drug -measure-hopes-for-drug-free-generation.html.

205 Mass incarceration of Black people: The Sentencing Project, "Crack Cocaine Sentencing Policy: Unjustified and Unreasonable," April 1997.

207 Charles Krauthammer invented the term *crack baby*: Charles Krauthammer, "Children of Cocaine," *Washington Post*, July 30, 1989.

207 no science to prove any of this: Washington, *Medical Apartheid*, 212–215; "'Crack Baby' Study Ends with Unexpected but Clear Result," *Philadelphia Inquirer*, July 22, 2013, http://articles.philly.com/2013-07-22 /news/40709969_1_hallam-hurt-so-called-crack-babies-funded-study.

CHAPTER 25: The Soundtrack of Sorrow and Subversion

213 Black men were the only ones producing major Black films: Guerrero, *Framing Blackness*, 157–167.

214 Clarence Thomas had been accused: Manning Marable, *Race, Reform, and Rebellion: The Second Reconstruction and Beyond in Black America, 1945–2006* (Jackson: University Press of Mississippi, 2007), 216–217; Earl Ofari Hutchinson, *The Assassination of the Black Male Image* (New York: Simon and Schuster, 1996), 63–70; Duchess Harris, *Black Feminist Politics from Kennedy to Clinton*, Contemporary Black History (New York: Palgrave Macmillan, 2009), 90–98; Deborah Gray White, *Too Heavy a Load: Black Women in Defense of Themselves, 1894–1994* (New York: W. W. Norton, 1999), 15–16.

214 stepped away from the Communist Party: Joy James, "Introduction," in *The Angela Y. Davis Reader*, ed. Joy James (Malden, MA: Blackwell, 1998), 9–10.

217 she proposed a "new abolitionism": Angela Y. Davis, "Black Women and the Academy," in *The Angela Y. Davis Reader*, 222–231.

217 the Violent Crime Control and Law Enforcement Act: Alexander, *The New Jim Crow*, 55–59; Marable, *Race, Reform, and Rebellion*, 218–219; Bill Clinton, "1994 State of the Union Address," January 25, 1994,

www.washingtonpost.com/wp-srv/politics/special/states/docs/sou94
.htm; Ben Schreckinger and Annie Karni, "Hillary's Criminal Justice
Plan: Reverse Bill's Policies," *Politico*, April 30, 2014, www.politico
.com/story/2015/04/hillary-clintons-criminal-justice-plan-reverse
-bills-policies-117488.html.

CHAPTER 26: A Million Strong

220 were intellectually inferior due to genetics or environment: Richard J.
Herrnstein and Charles A. Murray, *The Bell Curve: Intelligence and Class
Structure in American Life* (New York: Free Press, 1994), xxv, 1–24, 311–
312, 551; Dorothy E. Roberts, *Killing the Black Body: Race, Reproduction,
and the Meaning of Liberty* (New York: Pantheon Books, 1997), 270.

220 New Republicans issued their extremely tough "Contract with America": "Republican Contract with America," 1994, see http://web.archive
.org/web/19990427174200/ http://www.house.gov/house/Contract/CON
TRACT.html.

221 they tried, once more, to get Angela Davis fired: Marina Budhos,
"Angela Davis Appointed to Major Chair," *Journal of Blacks in Higher
Education* 7 (1995): 44–45; Manning Marable, "Along the Color Line:
In Defense of Angela Davis," *Michigan Citizen*, April 22, 1995.

222 The year 1995 was when the term *super predator* was created: B. W.
Burston, D. Jones, and P. Roberson-Saunders, "Drug Use and African
Americans: Myth Versus Reality," *Journal of Alcohol and Drug Educa-
tion* 40 (1995), 19–39; Alexander, *The New Jim Crow*, 122–125; John
J. Dilulio Jr., "The Coming of the Super Predators," *Weekly Standard*,
November 27, 1995.

222 it was flawed in its sexism: "Black Women Are Split over All-Male
March on Washington," *New York Times*, October 14, 1995.

223 A book of his commentaries was published: Mumia Abu-Jamal, *Live
from Death Row* (New York: HarperCollins, 1996), 4–5.

223 because of the protests, Mumia was granted an indefinite stay: "August
12 'Day of Protest' Continues Despite Mumia's Stay of Execution," *Sun
Reporter*, August 10, 1995; Kathleen Cleaver, "Mobilizing for Mumia
Abu-Jamal in Paris," in *Liberation, Imagination, and the Black Panther
Party: A New Look at the Panthers and Their Legacy*, ed. Kathleen Cleaver
and George N. Katsiaficas (New York: Routledge, 2001), 51–68.

223 pledged to lead "the American people in a great and unprecedented conversation on race": William J. Clinton, "Commencement Address at the University of California San Diego in La Jolla, California," June 14, 1997, Gerhard Peters and John T. Woolley, The American Presidency Project, www.presidency.ucsb.edu/ws/?pid=54268.

CHAPTER 27: A Bill Too Many

227 "The concept of race has no genetic or scientific basis": "Remarks Made by the President, Prime Minister Tony Blair of England (via satellite), Dr. Francis Collins, Director of the National Human Genome Research Institute, and Dr. Craig Venter, President and Chief Scientific Officer, Celera Genomics Corporation, on the Completion of the First Survey of the Entire Human Genome Project," June 26, 2000, https://www.genome.gov/10001356.

228 And that 0.1 percent difference between humans *must* be racial: Nicholas Wade, "For Genome Mappers, the Tricky Terrain of Race Requires Some Careful Navigating," *New York Times*, July 20, 2001.

230 President Bush condemned the "evil-doers": Marable, *Race, Reform, and Rebellion*, 240–243.

231 It once again put the blame on Black children: Marable, *Race, Reform, and Rebellion*, 247.

232 Barack Obama, subverted Cosby's message: "Transcript: Illinois Senate Candidate Barack Obama," *Washington Post*, July 27, 2004.

CHAPTER 28: A Miracle and Still a Maybe

235 He claimed to be exempt from being an "extraordinary Negro": Barack Obama, *Dreams from My Father: A Story of Race and Inheritance* (New York: Three Rivers Press, 2004), 98–100.

236 if southern Louisiana took "a direct hit from a major hurricane": "Washing Away," *New Orleans Times-Picayune*, June 23–27, 2002; Jessie Daniels, *Cyber Racism: White Supremacy Online and the New Attack on Civil Rights*, Perspectives on a Multiracial America (Lanham, MD: Rowman and Littlefield, 2009), 117–155; Naomi Klein, *The Shock Doctrine: The Rise of Disaster Capitalism* (New York: Metropolitan Books / Henry Holt, 2007).

239 spoke honestly about his feelings for a country that had worked overtime to kill him and his people: "Obama's Pastor: God Damn America,

U.S. to Blame for 9/11," ABC News, March 13, 2008, http://abcnews
.go.com/Blotter/DemocraticDebate/story?id=4443788.

240 Angela Davis, cast a vote for a major political party for the first time in
her voting life: "On Revolution: A Conversation Between Grace Lee
Boggs and Angela Davis," March 2, 2012, University of California,
Berkeley, video and transcript, www.radioproject.org/2012/02/grace-lee
-boggs-berkeley/.

242 Alicia Garza, Patrisse Cullors, and Opal Tometi founded #BlackLives-
Matter: "Meet the Woman Who Coined #BlackLivesMatter," *USA
Today*, March 4, 2015, www.usatoday.com/story/tech/2015/03/04/alicia
-garza-black-lives-matter/24341593/.

INDEX

Nathan Bajar

JASON REYNOLDS

is a #1 *New York Times* bestselling author, a Newbery Medal honoree, a Printz Award honoree, a National Book Award finalist, a Kirkus Prize winner, a two-time Walter Dean Myers Award winner, an NAACP Image Award winner, and the recipient of multiple Coretta Scott King Honors. He was the American Booksellers Association's 2017 and 2018 spokesperson for Indies First, and his many books include *When I Was the Greatest*, *The Boy in the Black Suit*, *All American Boys* (cowritten with Brendan Kiely), *As Brave as You*, *For Every One*, the Track series (*Ghost*, *Patina*, *Sunny*, and *Lu*), *Long Way Down*, which received both a Newbery Honor and a Printz Honor, and *Look Both Ways*. He lives in Washington, DC. He invites you to visit him online at JasonWritesBooks.com.